Forged
Made Strong in Weakness

SEAN NEAL

ISBN 978-1-63575-590-9 (Paperback)
ISBN 978-1-63575-591-6 (Digital)

Christian Faith Publishing, Inc.
296 Chestnut Street
Meadville, PA 16335
www.christianfaithpublishing.com

Printed in the United States of America

Contents

CHAPTER 1

Introduction

The July sun sat perched, perfectly atop idyllically shaped clouds; its rays permeating the thin layers, blurring the distinction between sun and shade. Beads of sweat form on the foreheads of onlookers. While initially gently warming, their skin now screams at the intensity of the heat. The lawn is filled with bystanders, family, and friends as they wait to cheer on their swimmers with vaunted anticipation. The faintest breeze bustles through the trees lining the edge of the viewing area, creating a fleeting reprieve. Shouts and cheers of encouragement and coaching fill the air; mixed with the ever present splashing and crashing of water creates a seemingly idealistic scene from the pages of everyday life.

"Eight and under boys, twenty-five-meter freestyle," a stark voice blares over the loud speaker.

In a frenzy, swimmers make their way to the pool. The water looks cool, crisp, and undisturbed like the quietness of a calm mountain stream. However, cooling off is the least of their worries. They are here to win, here to earn that prestigious blue ribbon.

It's the time of their lives; summer vacation in elementary school with boys that are closer than brothers, blood brothers. In principle, they'd fight to the bitter end, refusing to let each other down. In practice, it looked a lot more like rabble rousing and other mischievous antics, but those bonds remain taut, linking them together in years to come.

"Swimmer's up!"

Six young boys line up on the edge of the pool. Goggles adjusted, stances nailed, and faces set, determined to get off the blocks first. Analyzing their form and their apparent readiness; who's got the best chance to win? One can always discern the heart of a champion, often at a mere glance. It's written all over their face, like a freshly acquired sunburn. Granted, today's race is for fun, but ultimately winning is fun.

"Take your mark…"

All eyes rest on the final swimmer in lane five. Something is most assuredly different about this young man. He sits on the edge of the pool instead of standing like the others. His goggles are set and his game face is on, but surely he doesn't think he can gain an advantage by starting his swim in such a way. It goes against all logic. Without another moment's pause, the whistle blows and they're off.

With a splash, the swimmers hit the water and are propelled forward in a chaotic mix of flailing arms and frantic kicking. The strong separate themselves and edge out an early lead, while the swimmer in lane five falls behind.

Probably one of those kids who will get three quarters of the way down the pool and stand up resulting in disqualification.

One minute in and all swimmers have finished. They are out of the pool, dried off, and on their way back to the sidelines appearing content with their race performance; all except for the swimmer in lane five, who still has nearly halfway to go. At this point, something peculiar begins to take shape.

The cheering gets louder. Instead of fading off and parents losing interest they begin to focus. They move closer to the pool. They cheer and yell as the swimmer takes one stroke after another. He's slow, yet determined. He's last by a long shot, unabashed by the absence of other competitors. One stroke after another, his coach yells, "Pull! Pull! Pull! Pull!" as if he's in the race of his life, which unbeknownst to most, he is.

He reaches the shallow end, and surprisingly, he doesn't stand up and walk the final five meters. He doesn't look around at the other lanes, he doesn't stop; he just continues with steady stroke after steady stroke. He won't quit. He approaches the wall and with one final pull, touches it to end the heat.

His father grabs his arms and pulls him from the pool. He lifts him up and sets him down in his wheelchair. After wrapping up in his towel, he proceeds to greet his friends outside the pool with a grin rivaling Michael Phelps in his Gold Medal glory.

Leaving the pool, he inquires, "What was my time?"

They high five and congratulate him, swimmers and bystanders alike. The young boy doesn't realize the impact he's having on every person watching. This transcendent scene, these small town people, they get it. They value the can-do spirit, the sheer grit and determination.

Some deep revelations are held within the confines of that pool; most obviously to never quit, to never give up, and never let circumstances dictate what one does or who one becomes. It's about focus. It's about being our own biggest competitor. It's about being the best version of ourselves. It's about tackling each obstacle with the same fortitude and vigor regardless of the stakes. It's about gratitude, the love of a father, and building up those around us. It's about faith. It's about hope. It's about fighting the good fight and fulfilling our destiny.

You have likely discerned that the swimmer in lane five is me. Through the confines of this book, I hope to share with you the evolution of my nature, the forming of my character and the on-going progression of my relationship with and knowledge of our Heavenly Father. Woven throughout these pages are the lessons He is instilling in me, the strength He is building in me, and the ferocious tenacity for life He is developing in my heart.

My hope is the following pages will be an encouragement to you. That Jesus would speak through them into the depths of your soul and anchor you to Him. My hope is in seeing what He has done for me, how He is revealing Himself and how He is working in my life you will be built up, edified, drawn towards Him and prepared to tackle any obstacle that comes your way.

Further, that your heart and mind would be *forged* as mine have been. That it would be shaped through the heating, beating, and hammering of this life. That a bond would be constructed and deepened between you and the one who cares more about you than you could ever imagine; and that you would become a duplicate, an imitation, a reproduction of Him; His character and love. A genuine, authentic, bona-fide representation of who Jesus is. That you can see your life as being hammered by trials, heated and beaten by pressure and scorn, and refined and shaped by continued pursuit of His glory. Ultimately, Forged.

CHAPTER 2

This Isn't Normal

I sat perched on my haunches; my feet shoulder width apart.

"Come on, Sean. You can do it, buddy!" my dad encouraged. "Just stand up big guy."

At four years old, this was part of my daily routine. I was incentivized with a whole quarter for each time I rose from the depths of the carpet to a standing position.

Determined to make my dad proud, I put every ounce of strength into reaching that pinnacle. Leaning forward and placing the majority of my weight upon the balls of my feet I attempted to straighten my legs, elevating my body to an upright position.

"You almost got it, Sean!" Dad persisted as I stood with my upper body extended parallel to the floor.

Gritting my teeth and closing my eyes, I tapped every fiber of stored caloric energy and pushed myself upright. Placing my hands first on my knees, then on my thighs, and finally on my hips I was indeed standing.

"There." I said softly, content and somewhat winded. "I did it."

Proud, but always one to push the limits, even at a young age I continued. "I'm going to walk."

I gently lifted my right foot and prepared to take a step. Six inches ahead, I set my foot back down.

There, that wasn't so hard, I pondered.

Now was the tricky part. Leaning forward, I transferred more of my weight to my right foot. As I attempted to move my left foot forward and return to a stable standing position, my muscles failed. In a heap, I collapsed to the floor.

What is wrong with me, I groaned.

"Whoa! Nice job, Sean! You're going to be running before you know it." Dad said as he came to my aid.

Only I wasn't. Try as I might, this was not going to get better. I couldn't build muscle and no amount of exercise, physical therapy, protein powder, or supplements was going to change that. In fact, it was going to get worse. The older I grew, the weaker I would feel, the more severe my contractures would get, and the further away from normal my life would become.

Looking up at Dad, I could see the concern in his eyes. I could sense the apprehension in his disposition. Yet, he just smiled, patted me on the back, and handed me my quarter.

Six months earlier, my parents could no better offer an answer to the question, "What's wrong with me?" than I could in my four-year-old vocabulary. It was only evident something was amiss.

I was fortunate to be born into a loving family who cared deeply for me. My early childhood years were just like anyone else in small town America. I was born the only son to a third generation farmer.

A toe head blonde, my parents and sister were thrilled as I came into the world. Dreams filled their heads of who I might become and what I might accomplish. Endless potential; a state champion quarterback, a future neuro-surgeon, following in my father's footsteps as a farmer, any-thing was possible.

Early on, life appeared to be normal. Once I started walking however, it was obvious something was awry. I walked with a peculiar gait, waddling to and fro as if each step took more care and thoughtful purpose than it ought. At unpredictable and often inopportune times, I would tumble to the ground; my legs giving out from underneath me. As time progressed, the falling not only persisted and intensified, but even standing up became problematic.

My parents remained steadfast in hope and unrelenting in optimism. As we went from doctor to doctor, however, there were no answers and their minds were prone to ponder the worst-case scenario.

Following months of uncertainty, they decided the best course of action was to follow doctoral advice and proceed with a muscle biopsy; a procedure that would, if all went according to plan, facilitate a diagnosis.

In preparation for the surgery, we endeavored to stay positive.

"Mav, you got a bogey on your six!" Dad squelched behind his mask. "Break right, break right." he continued.

The Top Gun reference was assuredly lost on me, but nevertheless, I held the oxygen mask tight to my face.

In reality, we were practicing how to apply the orally administered anesthesia for my procedure later that morning, but in my mind, I was the squadron leader on a top-secret mission.

"He's coming around again. Line up on 'em and let him have it, Mav!"

My eyes narrowed and focused as the imaginary narrative took on a life of its own. My hands tightly gripped the loaner hospital toys. In my mind, it was no ring toss; it was the joystick of an F-14 fighter jet.

"Hammer down!" Dad softly bellowed, gently shaking my hands to mimic the effects of machine gun fire. "Bogey down. Good shootin' Mav!" He said patting me on the shoulder.

My dad and I were aviation enthusiasts, him more than me, as I was enamored by anything that moved and made noise, such is the case for most toddlers. But it was in moments like these that seeds of great optimism were planted deep in my heart, seeds that would grow into fruits of faith, persistence, and hope. Seeds that shortly after, though, would have their germination starkly threatened.

"Mr. and Mrs. Neal?" the doctor said as he entered following the surgery.

"I'm Dr. Bergen. Sean did very well, but I have some news I need to share with you."

He spoke flatly; his voice void of emotion, presenting his findings and analysis as perceived fact.

Their heart rates quickened. On one hand, they were anxious to learn of what condition plagued their son, but on the other, they were apprehensive of what the diagnosis might mean for the future.

"Sean has what's known as Spinal Muscular Atrophy or SMA." he paused.

With blank stares, my parents exchanged glances with one another unsure of the meaning behind those empty utterances.

"It's a genetic disease that attacks nerve cells, called motor neurons in the spinal cord," he continued, "it is these neurons that are responsible for communicating with voluntary muscles throughout the body; muscles that you and I control, such as those in the arms and legs. Depending on the severity and onset of the disease, it can affect walking, crawling, breathing, swallowing, as well as head and neck control."

As my parents would soon learn, genetic disorders such as SMA are caused by a mutation in a gene. Every person has two copies of each gene, one from each parent. A carrier is a person who has one normal gene and one abnormal gene. One normal gene is enough to mask the abnormal one and carriers are most of the time unaware they are indeed carriers. Approximately one in thirty-five people are a carrier of the mutated gene that causes SMA, as is the case for my parents.

Both being carriers, but otherwise symptom free and having no reason to suspect otherwise, they didn't give it a second thought. Even if they had known, in order for their child to have the disease manifest they'd both need to pass down his and her own copy of the abnormal gene; only a twenty-five percent chance. And I was the unlucky one in four who had the disease manifest.

Unsure of how to react and what to say, the only words they could muster were, "What does that mean?"

"Essentially, the body and organs continue to grow at a normal pace, while the muscles throughout the body do not. This leads to substantial weakness."

In his limited understanding of the disease, he tried to explain the resulting life for an affected person.

"It feels as though you know what you want your body to do, but never have the physical strength to accomplish it. It's like having a fifty-pound weight fastened to all of your extremities."

He paused, took a breath, and exhaled slowly as if the next words would be particularly hard to stomach.

"In these kinds of situations, the person afflicted often doesn't live past age ten."

A frigid silence fell over the room as the gravity of those words sank in.

Sadness and anger; fear and panic all came at once. This can't be happening. Not to us. Sure, children are diagnosed with life-threatening diseases every day, but not us. We aren't that family.

But we were. Denial or not, reality had just sucker punched them both.

Fortunately, for me, I have no memory of this time in my life. I had no awareness of what was going on around me and the time for the battle to be waged in my mind had not yet come. Regardless, the war was just beginning and the gaping wounds left by Dr. Bergen's empty words threatened to take their first casualty.

CHAPTER 3

The Mold

The drive home took place in complete silence. Words were so inadequate for the feelings welling up inside them. Numb. Numb to the world, numb to each other, they sat motionless. In stark contrast to their outward stoicism, their minds raced sporadically. Jumbled thoughts bounced around with such velocity, focusing on any one of them for longer than a few seconds was nearly impossible. There has to be a mistake. Sean is such a happy little boy. He's so full of life, so full of potential, but now his days are numbered?

The statement Dr. Bergen had declared with such matter of fact finality was completely void of hope. There must be more to find out. There must be knowledge he is unaware of. The burden is on us now, to find out, to research, and know with absolute certainty, what this disease means for our son.

As the leader and provider for our home, this burden fell heavier upon the shoulders of my father. His personality is of a rock; solid, adamant, and firm. He's a problem solver, yet, standing in the shower the next morning, the weight and burden came crashing down on him.

"This is my son." he cried out. "This isn't just anyone. Not just some kid down the street. He's a Neal. He's a part of the legacy of this family. Why?! Not my son! Take me. Let it be me!"

He pleaded in anguish to a silent universe.

The water continued to fall, drowning out the cries of his soul. With his forehead pressed against the outer wall, he closed his eyes, the hiss of the falling water filtering out everything around him.

Forming his hand into a fist, he began to hammer against the wall. Like the methodical beating of a war drum, his hand collided with the shower tiles. Thump. Thump. Thump. The sound reverberated back in apparent mockery.

For the first time, the full effect of his emotions ran their course. It had to be suppressed, he lamented. He had to be strong for his family; and while he himself was heartbroken, even this moment, in the shower, would need to be stricken from the record for years to come.

As his pleading continued in prayer, calling out to God for help, there came an ebbing, a slight lifting, and then a quieting. Clarity seeped in as the curtain of clouded sadness began to part. Like the softening winds of a tumultuous storm, this clarity offered a reprieve, but left no answers to all the questions.

His tears replaced by the stern gaze of a determined man caught up in the perfect will of God. In a moment riddled with darkness, it was clear what path he would take. He would make life work for his son, whatever that meant. He set his face like a flint, never to waiver, never to falter, but rather to be the figurative hands and feet his only son would need him to be.

While not knowing the extent to which it was true, he inherently understood the trials of this life would be many for me, and in those trials I would come to the end of myself. He would dig deep to be the unwavering support that would allow me to gain traction in my world.

He, and in essence my whole family, anchored and directed in the truth of Jesus could become the mold for my character. The cast, that one way or another was going to shape the outlook and ability of my life to become what it was meant to be.

From an outsider's perspective, the resulting attitude and determination resembled either blind optimism or faith filled assurance. Through prayer, my parents remained vigilant and determined to find out more about this disease.

Their hope would be rewarded. Their search would lead them to Doctor Crawford, and while three thousand miles away, he would serve as the light at the end of the tunnel.

He was considered an expert on the issue by many in the medical field and agreed to see me in Baltimore, Maryland. Upon consultation and review of my condition, he concluded I had one of the least severe forms of SMA and would "live to be a grandfather."

What an indescribable relief.

Thankfully, technological advances have come a long way in over two decades. Today, the testing is more accurate and attainable through a simple blood test. Additionally, knowledge has vastly increased allowing detection to occur prior to birth. Had the same knowledge existed upon my initial diagnosis, an untold amount of heartache and pain could have been avoided, knowing I could live a long, fulfilling life.

Regardless, at the age of two and a half, my life changed forever. Many hopes and dreams were shattered in an instant. In its simplest terms, this diagnosis meant that once my ability to walk faded, which it would, I'd be confined to a wheelchair for the remainder of my life. I would never ride a bike, never climb a tree, and I'd never play catch with my dad. What about the things in life that really mattered? Would I ever get married? Who would want to marry someone in a wheelchair? Would I be able to hold my own children? Would I be able to financially support a family? Would I be able to drive a car? All valid questions for which my parents had no answers.

In the midst of this perceived tragedy, however, a fighter was emerging. A warrior was being molded. A faith filled mindset was being forged in the fire. It was being hardened, purified, and cast into a weapon that could be used against discouragement; and until I could grasp it for myself, my parents found their path stretching out before them.

Out of heartbreak often comes victory; and once the choice was made to not let SMA be what defines me, we ran with it. There was no stopping, and my life would not be limited or held back because of disease. I was fortunate to not have my lifespan affected and was determined to live a full, blessed life.

CHAPTER 4

What's Wrong with Me?

Most would say a lot, evidenced most prominently by the wheelchair I sport on a daily basis. It's the first thing people notice about me and it's instantly part of my first impression. Most of the time people avoid the obvious question, but every now and then, a brave soul will inquire, what happened Sean? Why do you need a wheelchair?

Typically, I'll make up an elaborative narrative about a skydiving accident gone wrong or a deep-sea diving shark attack, but as you already know the truth, I'll spare you the gory details of a fictional tale.

In reality, we are all flawed in one way or another. We all have insecurities, bad habits we'd like to break, and attitudes we'd like to alter, disabilities if you will. Often, there's no way to change them, no way to predict what they will be, but most of us are very adept at hiding them. We put up walls to protect ourselves. We often hide behind thin veneers, the appearance of wholeness and happiness evidenced by our Facebook profiles, and the highlight reel of our Instagram feeds, yet we have struggles.

But what happens when we are rendered unable to conceal our biggest insecurity? What if stamped on our foreheads was the one thing we hope to keep hidden, even from those closest to us; a stamp in the form of a 250-pound wheelchair. No matter how much effort, time, and energy I put forth, it's surprisingly difficult to disguise. Granted, I could decorate it with tassels, ribbons, and bows, to rival a magical pixie horse; or better yet, I could paint it yellow and pretend I drive a dumpster truck every day, but it's still going to be just a wheelchair.

So let's get it out there. No, I cannot walk, not even to my seat on the airplane, Ms. Flight Attendant. Yes, I sleep in a regular bed. No, I don't drool. Yes, I need some assistance for many things in my life. And yes, my chair qualifies as a vehicle at the McDonald's drive thru. Well, they won't turn you away anyhow.

As a young boy, I had t-shirts I wore so often; they were discolored, faded, and practically wearing in two. Shirts that said, "Never quit, failure is not an option" and

"Never quit, never give up." Looking back, these were as much for my parents as they were for me. A reminder displayed in front of them every day that we weren't giving up. I wouldn't view myself differently than anyone else. I may have done some things differently, but I was not "disabled" and I did not want to be treated as if I were. If I deserved a punch from my friends, I got it. There was no special treatment, and if such was offered, it was staunchly rejected.

I didn't recognize it at the time, but refusing to acknowledge the reality of my situation presented major heartache when I wasn't in control of the mirror in front of me. There was nothing wrong with my attitude, but in being so different from the status quo, it wasn't easy to explain.

Pay phone clutched in my grip, I awaited the response of my parents.

"Please come get me!" I beseeched. "I hate it here. I just want to come home!"

Ah, summer camp. What a marvelous time. At eight, I was certainly old enough to attend and had stayed overnight at my friends' houses many times, but this was different.

"Sean, you have to stay there. You have a counselor. A lot of effort has gone into getting you there and making this a fun experience. Just go have fun. Go swimming in the lake or something." my mom encouraged in vain.

"No, I don't want to be here. I'm coming home, even if I have to drive my wheelchair all the way there."

That obviously wasn't going to happen. Sixty-five miles away, there's no way I'd make it even if I tried. In my brattish tirade, I was making life miserable for everyone around me.

"Fine!" I squawked hanging up the phone.

I bounded off lamenting my current predicament.

This was ridiculous. Here I was, in the most beautiful of locations. Camp Larson was the pristine embodiment of Lake Coeur'd Alene. A sprawling, manicured, camp with cabins, mess halls, the works. This week, it was home to the annual Muscular Dystrophy Association Summer Camp, a seven-day adventure with the sole purpose of providing enjoyment and fun for people, like me, with neuromuscular diseases.

Eyes still damp with tears, I looked up. There, a wheelchair; over there, another one; on the docks to the lake, even more of them. They were everywhere! I couldn't escape them! My mind raced rivaling that of an elephant trapped in a rubber mouse factory.

While I didn't have words to explain it at the time, what I hated, was not so much the presence of others in wheelchairs, after all I'm in one myself, but rather my distaste was for the metaphorical mirror being placed before my eyes. Everywhere I looked, there were people like me, confined to wheelchairs. Yet, I didn't see myself in that light. In my mind, I wasn't disabled. I didn't need nor want this camp, and I hated being forced to see my situation for what it truly was versus what I perceived it to be.

From my perception, I was Sean Neal, the son of a farmer, the kid who loves sports, the friend, the brother,

SEAN NEAL

and the jokester. Wheelchair bound or disabled was not anywhere near the words I would use to describe myself. I am not defined by this chair and therefore I don't belong here.

In reality, I did belong. I was just like every other camper there. I was set apart from the counselors and other "normal" people. There were two distinct groups; campers, those with disabilities, and everyone else; and regardless of what I believed, I did not belong in the "everyone else" category.

I was not handling it well; one could go a step further and even call me obnoxious, childish, immature, and cantankerous; and while that may sound harsh, it was accurate. I didn't handle it with grace or poise, but the concept is of great importance.

As I look back, it's plain to see I would've never been able to move beyond my circumstances, if they were all I saw. We can never rise higher than the vision we hold of ourselves in our minds eye. If we view and see lack, defeat, disease, despair, that's all we can hope to attain, but when we alter the paradigm to see victory, faith, life, success, and happiness, those are the things that come chasing us down.

I still refuse to look in the mirror and see myself in that light. Certainly, I am not averse to being around others with disabilities anymore. In fact, I take great pride and responsibility in encouraging others to alter their perception. To allow God to fully move in our lives, by viewing ourselves in His light, free of blemish, free of disease, free of iniquity, and watch Him take us places we've never dreamed of.

To the "natural" eye, there may be a list of things clinically awry, but so much of what's right *in* me is as a direct result of everything that's wrong *with* me.

CHAPTER 5

Dream Releasers

I've always felt the call of God was on my life. I've always known that somehow, someway, He was going to use me in a big way. It's an odd feeling. It's as though you're destined to do something, destined to make an impact, and yet unsure of how to get from where you are to where that place of impact is. Or even what that place of impact looks like. How do you know you've even arrived? It's not something I dwell on, but it's always there, and it inhibits me from just coasting through life. It's the reason I started motivational speaking, the reason I am writing this book, and the reason I can't walk through life merely hoping it'll all work out.

There's a certain credence that often comes with being in a wheelchair. Aside from combating mental retardation stereotypes, there's an assumption that you can get away with more. That people are more forgiving, understanding, and willing to more readily accept your faults and short-comings. It's true to a certain extent and while I won't negate perks like skipping lines at Disneyland and the occasional upgrade to first class, there's also an inherent downside.

Besides the obvious, not walking thing, I can never be anonymous. Wherever I go, I stand out like a sore thumb. Imagine the small town lore of "everybody knows every-body," only amplified to the point that everyone knows me, but likely, I don't know them.

My actions are watched, my reactions under greater scrutiny, and my decisions more easily judged as a result of increased visibility.

There is a purpose in my journey. Every decision I make and every action I take is calculated. It's taken with care and thought because there is such a longing in me to accomplish something greater than myself. It's rooted in my childhood. It was formulated in my upbringing and the people around me who had a profound impact upon my life.

The opening line in almost every speech I give is, "the most important thing you need to know about me is that God has blessed me immeasurably." It doesn't make sense. It's illogical for someone who obviously hasn't been dealt the greatest hand to say such a thing. Not only is it being said, but it's being professed and declared as a statement of faith. It's an attitude. It's evidenced by events, circumstances, and provision in my life, yet countered by an outward appearance contrary to what is typically perceived as normal. Second only to God, my family has been the most important thing in molding my life. They've embedded this mindset into the fabric of my character.

The grass was soft beneath me. As I sat, my skin gently warmed by the sun floating atop a perfect blue sky. The occasional cloud passed by casting the slimmest bands of shade over us. It was my sister, Annie's T-ball game. I sat on the sidelines watching with my parents at the ripe age of three. As I sat enjoying the summer sun, it happened.

First it appeared on Dad's thigh. He was lying down, the backpack we brought propping up his head like a pillow. He didn't notice it, but I sure did. It looked devious, malicious, and intent on causing harm. It moved slowly. Passing his waist, it stopped, perched on his shirt.

"You think you're something special, don't you?" I said internally with condemnation.

My pulse quickened. It wasn't next to skin, but it was getting close. Busy and occupied by the game Dad still didn't notice.

You're a confident little bugger, my mind persisted. My eyes began to bulge as the daddy long leg spider took more ill-intentioned steps towards his face.

The old wives' tale tells us that daddy long legs are some of the most venomous spiders in the world. However, in a cruel twist of fate, their fangs are too short to pierce the human skin and thus are harmless. I didn't come to know this tale as a fallacy until much later in life and for the purpose of this story the fact that there was a spider named "Gigantor" crawling around my dad was enough for this three-year-old to be more than slightly concerned.

Alright, it's just you and me mister spider, I thought furrowing my brow. Unwilling to let my hero fall prey to this creature of the dark, I mustered up all the strength I could. At this spry age, it wasn't much but in one quick sweeping motion I grabbed the spider with my bare hands, pinched, and chucked it as far as I could.

A bit confused, Dad looked down and asked, "You okay there, buddy?"

"Yeah, Dad! I'm good." I said, a proud confident smile occupying my face.

There was no way I was going to let a spider attack my dad. I admired him more than anyone. He was truly my hero and the man I wanted to be like more than anything. From day one, Dad has been the number one guy in my life.

Every young boy wants to be just like their dad when they grow up, and it was no different for me. My dad was strong, adventurous, hardworking, and got to drive big pieces of farm equipment all day long. What could be cooler?

He's a servant, a leader, and the hardest working man I've ever known. We've spent hours upon hours together in the combine and tractor. We talk about the farm, the future, about life, and our goals amongst other things. I've watched him work on farm equipment in the midst of a machinery breakdown and I've observed him as a caretaker of what's been entrusted to him. He takes great pride in every aspect of the farm. He does everything with a spirit of excellence and precision.

Add to it that I need a fair amount of assistance in my life; everything from getting dressed and showered in the morning to using the bathroom and changing position in bed in the middle of the night. My dad has primarily been the one to provide that assistance and never once has he complained. Never once has he done it begrudgingly. Never once has he asked for anything in return.

My biggest blessing is my family. I am fortunate to have grown up with two loving parents, a great sister, and an incredible supportive extended family. In a world where fatherless homes and divided families are often status quo, I realize my childhood was uncommonly good.

For most boys, running and playing, being active and busy is just a part of growing up. I instead developed deeper relationships with those around me. With increased time together came greater influence they had, which allowed me to rise above the circumstances in my life. It enabled me to see the favor and blessing of God in the midst of heartache.

My dad wasn't the only one who passed down attributes to me and formed the mold for my character. The first women in my life also played a pivotal role.

CHAPTER 6

The Women in My Life

"I can't believe you ate that pizza, Miles!" Colby said astonished.

"Yeah, that was crazy covered in all those peppers!" Garret added.

"I thought for sure you'd be running off to the bathroom before long." I quipped.

We had just left Pizza Hut and we were on cloud nine. It was Friday afternoon and we celebrating my fourteenth birthday. Annie was our chauffer and chaperone intent on making sure things didn't get out of hand. These were my blood brothers. The boys I had grown up with since day one and there's no one else I would rather be spending this day with. Miles, Garret, Colby, Dakota, and Trey. The six of us were inseparable and this birthday outing was no different.

We anxiously talked about what we'd do first upon arriving home. We'd been looking forward to this day for weeks; and now, it was finally here. There'd be video games, poker, some good movies, and of course lots and lots of food. Upon arriving at the house, we barreled out of the car, grabbed our things and made a mad dash inside. Once there it was a beeline straight to my room where Halo surely awaited.

"Sean, you painted your room?" Colby questioned.

"Um, I don't think so. Not that I know of."

I raised a peculiar glance as I caught up to him in the hallway. Truly, it hadn't been that long since he'd been at my house, and even so my room has never been painted.

As I peeked around the corner, I could unmistakably see my room was vastly changed. The walls were painted a deep maroon color. My bed was adorned with a new rustic style bedspread. My favorite sports posters were now framed and meticulously arranged on the walls. There was new shelving, and new pictures of my friends and family. It looked like something straight out of a magazine. It was nothing short of immaculate, its theme reminiscent of an old cabin in Alaska. Hints of rustic décor mixed with modernized comforts. It was perfect. Unbeknownst to me, my mom had done a complete makeover to my room for my birthday and I absolutely loved it.

She and I often watched those home makeover television shows and I always thought how cool it would be to have a surprise like that. To come home and have your "space" transformed from drab and rather ordinary to something new and unique and that's exactly what she had done.

I was blown away. We all anticipate gifts on our birthdays, but she had taken it to another level. She had spent all day putting it together and some untold hours planning and gathering the needed supplies. I was beyond blessed and my friends were here to experience it with me.

"Thank you, Mom!" I offered genuinely. "This is awesome!" I added as we embraced.

My mom is the most giving, compassionate woman I've ever known. Like my dad, she's a servant, but in a different way. She's helped with my care, always made sure that I had food to eat, and always encouraged me. She has an uncanny ability to be empathic. Her grace and mercy for others is unmatched. She's an expert at offering hospitality and exudes understanding in everything she does.

As many moms are, she's my biggest fan. She'd be the mom to come cheer me on in a math contest where all I had done was take a written examination. No, that never happened, thankfully, but her heart is content to support and encourage regardless.

How could I grow up in this kind of environment, with parents like these and not have their traits rub off on me? Add to that the component of being around them more as a result of my disability. You can see why many of those characteristics are so deeply engrained in me; that heart to serve, to lay down my life wholly and completely for another, the desire to lead and live with a spirit of excellence, the compassion and empathy for others.

We all have attributes passed down to us from our parents. Traits that are desirable and some that aren't. What's different here is to think what life would've been like without strong, God-fearing, encouraging people in my life. Having a child with a disability is a burden on everyone. There's a higher divorce rate among couples with a disabled child, there's undue financial stress, not to mention the psychological effects on the family.

I can't begin to think what my life would've been like if I had been born into a family with an absent father, or a family with a non-compassionate mother, or a family who simply didn't have the strength to push forward in spite of the odds. My parents are often complimented on how they've persevered through our situation saying if I had been their child, they wondered if they could've done the same, or if regrettably they would've put me in some kind of home.

What an existence that would be. Confined to a bed all day. No hope of a life. No future to look forward to. Merely existing, slowly fading away until one day it's all over. Even if it had been a supportive family, but those who lacked hope, it could've been disaster. I could've been a depressed, unmotivated, disinterested, bitter, angry at the world type of person with no ability to better those around me. But that isn't the future God had in mind for me. His favor existed on my life before I was even born. He knew He could trust my parents. He knew exactly how they'd react. He knew that they were equippers, enablers, encouragers, and motivators. He knew that they would thrust me into my destiny.

Just as important as my parents was my partner in crime, Annie.

"Come up here!" I hollered down to my sister.

At the top of our swing set, I awaited as she climbed the ladder to the platform. It was a four by four-foot landing bordered by a railing with openings for the ladder and slide. We had countless adventures on this slide including placing the baby pool at the bottom adding some water from the hose and making our own version of wild waters.

Today was much less adventurous as it were. It was a cool fall day and in an attempt to soak up the final rays of the season we were making the most of the afternoon. Suddenly, I felt the urge to use the bathroom. I was around four years old and was just discovering there are certain parts of the male anatomy that make going to the bathroom much more enjoyable. There was filling the toilet with bubbles, writing your name in the snow, and most importantly, anywhere was a suitable bathroom. The possibilities were endless, quite possibly too endless.

"You ready to go down the slide, Sean?" she asked.

"No, I want to stay up here."

I had to go, but knew if I went down the slide and hence inside the house, I wouldn't be coming back out.

"You go first. I have to go to the bathroom."

"I'll go down and tell Mom." she offered.

At four, I crawled nearly everywhere I went. I could still stand, but not well and coming inside from the play set would be much easier with Mom's help.

As she went down the slide, I got an idea, a terrible and wonderful idea. With a grin rivaling that of the Grinch, I decided to proceed.

I prepared myself for action. Once Annie reached the bottom of the slide, she stopped and paused as she prepared to call for Mom. I adjusted my position, changing trajectory, and accounting for wind speed I let it fly. 3...2...1... Bull's eye!! A perfect stream splashed down squarely on the crown of her head.

"Mom!" she screamed. "Sean peed on my head!"

She darted off towards the house, reality still setting in.

No longer needing to use the bathroom, I sat down atop the play set; content that my plan was an overwhelming success, yet cautious of the assured coming retribution.

Somehow, she forgave me. Regardless of my pride in this moment, she was my first best friend and my closest confidant to this day. We'd play for hours together; Nintendo 64, Barbies—yes, I played with Barbies—Legos, movies, you name it; we did it together. She is full of joy and quirkiness in an endearing way. She elicits a smile in everyone she meets and is the kindest, most inclusive, most generous, person I know. She was my second mom growing up, a role she often relished, and while we had our moments like most siblings do, we always have each other's back in the stiffest of battles.

I could go on and on; story after story indicative of the blessing my family has and continues to be. Not just my parents and my sister, but my grandparents, cousins, aunts, uncles, brother in law, and nieces, all of them in their own way have given a piece of themselves to spur me forward. In areas where I lacked, they were quick to contribute, slow to apprehension, and have always been my biggest fans.

See, my family members are dream releasers. They are, in the simplest form, the unmerited favor of God evidenced in my life. I did nothing to deserve it. I did nothing to earn it. Yet, He placed me where He knew I would flourish.

This kind of burden couldn't be placed on just any family. It would destroy a lot of homes, but instead of desolation, it has been a launching pad for faith. It's a real life demonstration of who Jesus is and what His favor looks like in this world.

We all have dreams stored up deep inside of us and there are certain people gifted at releasing those dreams. They have a way of understanding our very nature and instinctively knowing that the dream inside of us releases one to be the person we were created to be. In a way, we'd never be able to do on our own, they have a way of finding the inner potential that we possess.

They have a way of breaking through the barriers, breaking down the walls of insecurity we didn't realize were there and in one smooth motion, take us from a place of saying "that'll never be me" to Russell Wilson's infamous declaration of "Why not us?"

Because of the benefits accrued to me, it is my desire that everyone should look for and find the dream releasers in your life. Find the people who spur you on, who support, motivate, and encourage. It may not be your parents. It may not even be a family member, but find the people who push you towards your destiny. Take time to realize that these people are in your life for a reason. Be thankful for the demonstration of God's favor in your life. Slow down and take time to reflect on who you are because of them, and how your life would be undoubtedly different without their love, care, and support.

CHAPTER 7

Why Me?

Lying there, alone, on the hard asphalt, my mind raced. My biggest concern was who would come home first. Sure, Dad would see me and help, but my sister? I wasn't so sure. I could already see it; distracted by her loud music and pre wedding scatterbrain, driving right by or worse, right over me. I lay a mere six feet off the edge of the residential street that lined the front of our house.

"Mom!" I bellowed at the top of my lungs. "Help! Somebody, Anybody!"

I screamed with everything I had, but it was no use. No one could hear me. My mom was the only one home.

Busy upstairs preparing for my sister's wedding, the sound of my voice surely drowned out by the boisterous droning of the carpet cleaners.

It was the perfect storm. On a whim, I had decided to drive my wheelchair downtown to our farm shop where Dad was surely working on some interesting piece of equipment, a trip I had made many times. As I made my way down our driveway, I increased to top speed, approximately seven miles per hour.

The sun was shining brightly, and at around 11:30 a.m., I needed my sunglasses. As I neared the end of our driveway, I reached down to grab them. In doing so my drive hand slipped from my joystick. My wheelchair stopped on a dime, but being unrestrained by the absence of my seatbelt I kept moving and in a tuck and roll maneuver, worthy of a free runner, landed on the concrete, unable to move.

I could see my cell phone neatly tucked in the pouch of my wheelchair, but it was too far away to reach and I couldn't move to bring it closer. At first, relieved that I was otherwise not in pain, I felt relaxed. Someone would find me sooner or later. The sun is warm and nice. In fact, I'll just chill and take a nap.

That moment of calm evaporated as quickly as I had exited my chair and was consequently replaced by panic.

"Help! Someone, help!" I screamed in vain.

Embodying the definition of helpless, I spent the next twenty minutes bellowing at the top of my lungs. Scared, nervous, and feeling totally alone, I tried to pray but found little solace. The words filling my mind were "Why me?"

I can't begin to tell you how many times I've asked myself that question. How many times I've envisioned my life as "normal." What my life would look like and how all the troubles I experience would suddenly be nonexistent if I didn't have this wheelchair. I'd go on more dates, I'd have the perfect physique, I'd drive a better car, I'd have a better job, and quite assuredly, I wouldn't be lying here alone at this very moment.

Here I was, that question, "Why me" amplified in my palpable vulnerability.

Seriously. No one has driven by? This is ridiculous. I said knowing there were no ears close enough to hear. People drive by here all the time and the one day I could really use them; no one shows up.

What do you do when you're in a place of despair and panic wrought with fear? Do you angrily scream bloody murder? The outward screams an inadequate projection of the cries taking place within the confines of ones' inner being. I was furious. Angry that I was alone, upset that I was scared, and maybe most of all fuming that facing a situation such as this was even a reality to me.

Minutes later, unable to see much of anything other than the hunk of metal that is my wheelchair, I heard a rustling, a noise that resembled the opening of a sliding glass door. To my relief, the next sound to reach my ears was the sweetest of sounds. A full blown orchestral symphony, accompanied by Yo Yo Ma would have been mere pennies in comparison to the peace overtaking me as a result of the voice of my mother.

"Sean!?" She echoed with concern as she rushed towards me.

At this point, we undoubtedly experienced emotions at opposite ends of the pendulum. As my heart and mind were overflowing with relief and security, knowing my ordeal was over. Her horror had just begun. Her worst nightmare had come to fruition.

Any parent wants to protect their child from heartache and pain, a desire amplified when that child is faced with a situation such as mine. As she ran towards me, the chair blocking most of her view, only my limp legs and feet were visible to her.

Had I died? What injuries had I sustained? How long had I been there? What panic and stress had I endured, wondering when I would be found?

Simply relieved I hadn't been left alone on this earth, I offered no retort to her inquires, only a labored "Mom?" as she made her way over to me.

She knelt down silently in her nurse programmed methodology, assessing the situation. I was essentially uninjured; a couple of scrapes and bruises, but nothing major. I would be sore in the morning, but other than the emotional trauma, I was unaffected.

She wiped the blood from my forehead, the horror now replaced with compassion, wrapped her arms around me in a move that would give her almost as much comfort as it did me.

As she assisted me up to a sitting position, the only word to cross my lips was a single expletive. In that moment, it was the only word that captured both my sense of relief, but also my complete disdain for what had just occurred.

Minutes later accompanied by a neighbor, who had undoubtedly heard the ruckus, I was lifted back into my chair. For me, the worst had passed; but for Mom, that scene would replay over and over in her mind.

She couldn't protect me from any hurt that may come my way. No parent can. And as much as the encore presentation persisted her head, she found herself facing the same question I was, why me? Why our family? Her heart hurt for me in a way I will probably only fully understand after having children of my own.

As I contemplated the situation later, I found myself confused.

I thought that once I made the choice to live above my circumstances and focus on Jesus, life would be easy. One would hope and want to believe that in making a declaration of faith, suddenly the cares, troubles, and what ifs of the world around us would fade away. Our minds and hearts would be fixed on Him; we'd rejoice in the blessed assurance of hope in the future. Why wasn't that my reaction?

Jesus wants us to rest in Him, to be at peace, to walk out our lives without worry. He has it all figured out, and yet we still fear. We become anxious. We ask the question, why me? Why couldn't it be anybody else?

This wasn't the first time I had posed that question to myself. In fact, it was far from it. The most recent time, sure, but in all honesty not even the most vivid.

CHAPTER 8

I Just Want to Play the Game

I looked down at the basketball in my hands. Seated in my chair midway between the half court line and three-point line, I looked around at the empty gym. Bringing my face forward again, I looked up to the rim, my gaze narrowing upon the nylon net draped so effortlessly below.

Closing my eyes, I could feel the roughness of the leather as in spun past my fingertips. Catching it once again, that same roughness made smooth in the rotation of the ball as I forcefully pushed it down again. The soft methodical thud, thud, thud of the ball as I dribbled, drowned out as the once empty gym was now filled with adorning fans, cheering on their hometown squad, propelling them with every ounce of encouragement towards title glory.

I could see my teammates blanked by defenders as the clock inched closer to zero. Holding my hand high above my head I shaped it into a fist while simultaneous calling out "Ball side!" A play perfectly designed to not only break down this two-three zone, but ideally, facilitate an open shot for me or my teammates.

As I waited for the screener to set his feet, I lowered my stance. Bending my knees and crouching slightly lower, I prepared to execute the play with idealized perfection. I inched ever closer to the screener as the clock continued to tick down. Moving directly beside the screen, I shed my defender and faced with the slimmest of openings set my feet in a quick stop maneuver and elevated to shoot.

With my elbow tucked in tightly, I began to rise in a perfect line; not moving side to side, not shifting forward or backward, but a straight up ascension, my eyes fixed on the back of the rim. As I reached the top of my jump, I extended my shooting hand and at the same time, ever so slightly released the grip of my guide hand. The ball gently rolled off the tip of my finger.

I kept my gaze locked on the back of the rim as I descended back towards the court. Holding my follow through as I waited for the "swish," I softened the impact of my return to the ground with a slight bend of my knees. Still holding my follow through, I slowly inched backwards knowing instinctively that I had made the shot. The ball slowly entered my frame of vision, still with perfect back-spin. As it dropped through the net, the buzzer sounded.

This was the moment I had waited for all my life. In small town America, sports are a big deal. Every young child fantasizes about it and finds themselves star struck by the biggest celebrities they know, donning the court every Friday and Saturday night. I was no different and awaited the day with great eagerness and excitement for my moment in high school.

"Sean!" I was awoken from my trance. "Time to go. I have to lock up the gym." Bill, the custodian, chimed in.

I looked down at the ball still in my hands. Unable to muster the strength to even lift it above my head, I was back in reality. My daydream had abruptly ended.

"Okay." I offered back. "I'll be right there."

Unable to participate in the way I would've liked, I acted as manager. Longing to be involved in any way I could with the sport that was more than just an activity to me. It was my dream, my passion, and my pinnacle. And yet I had to just watch. Our team was decent, but we lacked something. We lacked a true leader; someone who when everything was going wrong would pull the team together. Our coach was phenomenal; a man who got every ounce of talent from his players, but we needed that floor general to dictate tempo and take the game to the next level. There was a missing piece.

As hard as it was at times, I always put on a smile, went to practice every day and watched my friends do the very thing I would give anything to do. The pain I experienced as I watched so many of them take it for granted surpasses comprehension. Some were lazy, uncommitted in their drills, and at times even halfhearted in their approach. They had everything I'd ever wanted and were just casting it aside.

If I had the ability to walk, this would be no different, I pondered. Just me and an empty gym would be a common occurrence. I knew that in order to be great, it took two things; repetition and vision. Being the first one here and the last one to leave epitomized that repetition and devotion and on the other hand, my visualization, my inner "daydream" reflected my vision. Only it wasn't just a daydream. I was seeing everything I would do on the court manifested in my mind and heart.

Sports are so mental. So much of the game is in your own mind. It's about confidence in your abilities. It's about playing with heart. It's about executing every play like it's your last, every possession as if you're down by two in the final minute of the state championship game. It's an attitude of success. It's visualizing every play, every move, every component and mechanic of your game and seeing the ball fall through the net in your mind before you ever step on the floor.

I had the mental part figured out. I wanted to be that player pushing everyone else to be better, giving 110% on every drill, scrimmage, line set, and free throw. And when it came to the game, I'd be the first player to dive, body extended into a crowd of people to save a loose ball.

To make matters worse, I knew sports were in my blood. My dad was a star player in high school, and my grandfather was a great athlete as well, he even boxed in college. My cousins were all phenomenal athletes; the go to players on their teams. Even my sister was a gifted athlete. The ability was in me, just not manifested. It's one thing to desire and long for talent and athletic ability, it's another to know it's in your genetics, but you just can't access it.

As I lay in bed, night after night, tears of agony rolling down my cheeks I prayed.

"God, why me? There are billions of people in this world. Why did you pick me? Why!?" I was angry. I was hurt. I was confused and full of despair.

I'm sure you can relate. It's probably not basketball, but perhaps questions of: Why do I have to be the one diagnosed with cancer? Why do I have to be lonely? Why do I have to deal with rejection? Why do I have to be the one to raise these children on my own? There are a lot of other people out there, who seemingly don't have this burden, who don't have this weight to carry, who seem to have it so easy. Why do I have to be the one to live this life?

The more I reflect and the older I get, the more I am convinced that the answer to "why me" is more simple than I would've initially expected. It's because He knew He could trust me, and in your case, you. He knew you were strong. He knew you could bear this burden and come out stronger on the other side. He knew you wouldn't quit. He knew the right people would be there to encourage you. He knew you would pull yourself up, dust yourself off and say to the storm, "Is that all you got?"

He made you. He formed you and says that you are beautifully and wonderfully made. Yet, He trusted you enough to give this burden at this appointed time, designed to ultimately thrust you into your destiny.

I often think about Job. Here's a man who God was bragging about to the devil. He was saying in effect, "Look at my servant, Job. Look how faithfully he serves me. He is a blameless and upright man." Yet, God allowed Satan to attack Job, testing his faithfulness. And as a result, Job lost everything; his family, his children, his possessions and everything he held dear. Through it all he remained strong and faithful. After which, God blessed him with double of what he had before his trials began.

The trials in Job's life happened only because God allowed them to. You can be firm and adamant that any troubles you encounter are only in your life because God allowed them to be. You can be hopeful and peaceful knowing that, "In all things God works for the good of those who love Him, who have been called according to His purpose" (Rom. 8:28). That includes the burdens, the trials, and the sorrow. All of it will work together for your good, for your future.

What if God is bragging about you? What if God is saying look at Sarah, look at Cameron, and look at Rachel. See how faithful they are to me. See how they serve me with their whole heart. With you, I am well pleased. What if you are being tested? What if God is allowing you to go through trials and struggle because you are an example like Job?

It changes our whole perspective if our troubles, our burden, our weight to carry are as a result of God bragging about us. It makes it bearable. It makes us want to serve Him even more. To glorify Him even more in our troubles. Don't let Him down. Be deserving of God's bragging.

Pass the test. Persevere through it all. Keep honoring God with your life. Keep putting Him first and get ready for the blessing He is going to pour out over you. This is but for a time. It too shall pass. Stand firm in your faith and in the midst of your "why me?" be like the Psalmist and say, "I believe that I shall look upon the goodness of the Lord in the land of the living! Wait for the Lord; be strong and take courage; wait for the Lord!" (Pss. 27:13–14).

CHAPTER 9

The Worst Day of My Life

I woke up. Squinting, I struggled to keep my eyes open. I couldn't make out much more than vague shapes and muffled sounds. Where was I, I wondered. The room was quiet and sterile feeling. There were no voices, but the presence of others emanated throughout the room. Before I could give it more thought, the pain hit me. Not striking sharp pain, but severe discomfort. I was unable to move. I tried to roll onto my side, but no longer had the physical strength to do so. I groaned in pain.

What was this excruciatingly hard surface I was laying on? Why does it feel as though my back is superglued to a piece of wood? Why can't I move? And where is my family? My mind raced.

I heard a voice. It was soft and comforting, yet instructive and firm.

"Lay still, Sean." she insisted. "You're in the recovery room."

"Is it over?" I asked, suddenly realizing through a mixture of recollection and process of elimination that I had just come out of surgery.

"Yes," she assured, "you did great. Just lay still."

"Can I see my parents?"

"They're waiting for you. You'll see them in your room soon. Just rest now."

Content with her answer and forced with no other choice than to accept it, I tried to fall back asleep. Just rest a few more minutes and when I wake up, I'm sure I'll be more comfortable. The past twelve hours of surgery evidently flew by, so an hour or so in the recovery room, should be nothing.

I wanted to move so badly. My back felt like nothing I had ever experienced. It was stiff and rigid; immobile, as if someone had placed my upper body in a concrete mold for the past day and a half, let the concrete set, placed me between two other, equally as hard, concrete blocks, and asked me to rest. Put another way, it felt as if a cabinet had been built around my midsection. A cabinet barely big enough to fit around my upper body, then forcefully stuffed my head through a hole in the top and closed the door.

Sleep was not going to happen. There was no way I could fall back asleep with this kind of discomfort regardless of the lingering effects of the anesthesia.

"Can I please move?" I pleaded. "This hurts and I am really uncomfortable."

"Hold on, sweetie," the voice in the room answered.

I could hear the shuffling of feet as another nurse made her way over to me. Grabbing the sheet underneath me the two gently turned me on my left side.

"Ah." I exhaled, as the new position seemed to alleviate some of the discomfort. My vision was much clearer now, removed from the bright lights overhead. I still couldn't make out any faces, nor turn my neck to attempt to, but I could see, what I assumed to be a middle-aged woman standing next to me in a light blue gown of some kind. A color that elicits no comfort what so ever, I might add. You'd think hospitals would pick something more soothing than white and "barely blue" to garb their nurses with, but I suppose in my frail, freshly carved open state, no color is particularly pacifying.

My respite was short lived, however, as the pain returned as quickly as it left. I wanted to move again. Over the next half hour, I turned from side to side three times. If I had been given my way, it would've been at least twice that, but hesitant to move me too much, the nurses negated my persistent requests.

After another half an hour of positional appeals it was time to move me to my hospital room. A team of three nurses wheeled a gurney into the recovery room. They gathered around me and using the same sheet that remained underneath me from before transferred me to the gurney. I was wheeled out the door, down the hall, and into the elevator. A brief moment later, I was on the third floor and headed toward my room. Once inside, I was transferred again, using the same method as before onto the hospital bed.

"Sean, it's Mom and Dad," my parents offered. "You did great bud! It's all over now."

Unable to respond and still not completely lucid, I was incredibly comforted by their voices. They were just as helpless as I was when it came to relieving any of my pain and discomfort, but merely being in the presence of their love, care, and encouragement was overwhelmingly reassuring.

As I woke the following morning, the effects of the anesthesia finally wearing off, I began to take account of my surroundings. It all came back to me. The single bed hospital room directly across from the nurse's station suddenly familiar again. The small wall mounted television softly recounted the day's headlines courtesy of Matt Lauer and Katie Couric of the Today show, a morning staple in the Neal home. The window seat to my right, the small table and chairs next to the door, and the abundance of wires and tubes stretching out from and around me all came into focus.

I had checked into the hospital three days ago and had now spent my second night at Shriner's Hospital in Spokane, Washington. I wasn't thrilled to be here, but was reminded of its "necessity" through the cacophony of voices in my head declaring with unmitigated confidence that it had to be done.

Another unfortunate side effect of my pal, Spinal Muscular Atrophy, I thought. Why not add scoliosis to the list of challenges to overcome? It would only make sense that with general muscle weakness, the proximal muscles of the trunk and midsection would lack strength as well, but it's not the most obvious of side effects.

Thankfully, we had put the surgery off as long as possible; a full-length spinal fusion. It consisted of placing titanium rods on either side of my spine, straightening it, and fastening it to the rods with wire and bone grafts. It was no small task and the rods, anchored in my pelvis with the aforementioned bone grafts, would run all the way up to the base of my neck. Any further growth in my back would be immediately stopped, and while I didn't know it yet, many of the aspects of daily life would become infinitely more challenging.

Dr. Bronson was a great doctor, however. He had put it off as long as possible. Another doctor I saw on a semi-regular basis would've had my back filleted open by age eight, but Dr. Bronson took a much more conservative approach.

He was a handsome and tall man, standing at six foot two with short brown hair. He had a calmness about him; soft spoken, but confident in his words. He was in his mid-thirties and was a rare mix of experience and compassion, optimistic, yet grounded. He had been reassuring over the past few years that my spine was still flexible and we needn't rush into a surgery of this magnitude. However, in recent months, my spine had begun to harden; and if we waited any longer, its flexibility could foreseeably be gone, resulting in a less than optimum surgical result.

At eleven years old, I would've given anything to avoid it. In fact, not two days earlier after checking into the hospital, I attempted to run away. After meeting nurses, anesthesiologists, Broom Hilda, as she called herself, an eccentric respiratory therapist, and numerous other supporting hospital staff that would be present throughout my recovery in the hospital, we left for the evening. It was our final evening away from the confines of the hospital.

After checking into our hotel, we met up with my aunt and uncle for dinner and a movie. Attempting to infuse humor and positivity into the midst of a dark situation, we watched Finding Nemo. A great movie; yet, unsurprisingly, I found myself distracted the entire time. I wasn't the only one not totally engulfed by the film; and instead, preoccupied by the reality of what would occur very soon.

After the movie, we walked out into the lobby; as my family visited with each other, I saw my chance and I took it. Going as fast as I could I made my escape, not really sure where I was headed. I was too scared to ride the elevator by myself back down to the exit of the mall, but I kept going despite the voices of my parent's calling.

"Sean! What are you doing? Where are you going?"

I knew I wasn't getting far, but I had to make an attempt. I had to show my sheer disapproval for the situation. I had to exhibit in some form my willingness to go under, over, around, or beside the giant that stood in my path.

I wasn't just running physically; I was running away in my mind. I was terrified. I felt alone and trapped. Surgery wasn't new to me, but that was all the more reason to be apprehensive. I knew what it felt like. I knew there was certain pain to be endured and the recovery would be long and laborious. What I didn't know was how it would affect my life and my future, which is perhaps, what scared me the most.

I didn't say much the rest of the evening. My dad, of course, caught up with me and led me back to the elevator lobby where my family waited. We exchanged pleasantries. Everyone wished me good luck, to which I accepted graciously with a smile and a thumbs up, despite my every inclination to be cynical, and we parted ways. Once back at the hotel, I changed clothes, got into bed, and went to sleep.

CHAPTER 10

The Time Has Come

I woke the next morning knowing everything was about to change. My attitude was less than ideal as we got ready for the day. My dad, presumably looking for encouragement and hope, turned the television to TBN, a Christian broadcast network as we dressed and readied ourselves. In the midst of the broadcast, the televangelist quoted a verse that would become the anthem for the rest of my life; a verse that would give us all hope. It was a glimmer of light in the darkest of nights.

"Now unto Him that is able to do exceedingly, abundantly, above all that you could ask or think according to the power that worketh in us" (Eph. 3:20). I could tell you my attitude changed immediately. That I recognized the love of God and had complete peace about what was happening, but that wouldn't be further from the truth.

In reality, it was encouraging. It was a glimmer of hope, but it encouraged my parents more than anything. It gave them strength to go on, strength to press forward in what they knew had to be done. That's not to say it didn't speak to me, because it did. And now, being older, I can see the favor God was demonstrated in that moment, but at the time, it wasn't some revelation imparted on me.

It wasn't a get out of jail free card. I still had to go through it. I still had to endure the pain. I still had to be sliced open and operated on. I still had to be stuck with needles, given IV's, an epidural, a catheter, a potential blood transfusion, and years of recovery before I would regain some resemblance of normal. In spite of it all, there was hope, however. This scripture provided an anchor to hold onto, a promise of better days, and a rested assurance that God was with me.

Favor isn't always smooth sailing. It doesn't necessarily mean all our troubles go away. It doesn't always take the form of provision, or smiles, or joy. Sometimes the favor of God is the strength to go on; the hope of better days, knowing that God is with you. It's in the form of courage; resiliency to face the storm and say, "Do your worst." Sometimes, it's not even that *robust*, but it's strength enough to stand and endure the fight. To stand, lift your head and stare down the giant before you.

Later that morning we drove back to the hospital and checked in for good. We would be staying the night and the next time I went through these hospital doors; I would be different. I would be changed and on the other side of this metaphorical mountain.

The day was filled with more tests, blood draws, hospital tours, and general familiarity with what would take place over the next week. Still less than thrilled with the situation, and it didn't get any better as another hospital employee entered the room.

"Hi, Sean," she said as she entered. "My name is Carrie Williams. I will be doing some testing on you today, to prepare us for tomorrow morning."

"Hi." I responded shyly.

"We are going to do what's known as Intraoperative Neurophysiological Monitoring." she started to explain. "I am going to hook up several wires and nodes and attach them with tape to different nerves on your body. This will allow us to get a baseline, so during your surgery tomorrow I can monitor them and detect any injuries to nerves before they become so severe they cause defects after the operation."

"Okay." I replied, a bit skeptical.

Carrie methodically took small quarter size nodes, connected a wire to each one, and began to place them on different areas of my body. She then connected the other end of the wire to an electrical device used to monitor the nerves.

"This will be much faster tomorrow," she continued, "the first time is always the slowest, most painstaking, but we will re-apply all of these immediately prior to your surgery in the morning."

I didn't respond. I was growing increasingly bothered by the whole process as she continued to apply node after node, and the inevitability of surgery became more real with every passing second. After approximately twenty minutes, I was all connected and looked like something out of a horror film, Frankenstein or even more accurately a robot in prototyping as the wires dangle loosely away from the outer shell of the body.

"Let's get a picture, Sean." my dad offered trying to make light of the situation and hoping I would similarly see the humor.

I smiled sardonically. Not exactly the reaction he was hoping for.

I missed it. I missed an opportunity to show the love of God to everyone around me. Here I was, looking like Iron Man in his early stages, looking like a robot, like a cyborg of some kind, and I couldn't get out of my own head. I could've had so much fun with it. I could've taken a moment and transplanted all of us out of the reality and heaviness of the situation, but I couldn't get beyond my own perceived misery. It wasn't painful. It wasn't uncomfortable, but I wouldn't make an effort to look for the good in a situation.

How often do we do that to ourselves? We're not where we want to be, but we can still look for the best. We can still choose life and optimism, but instead we focus more intently on ourselves and sink into a puddle of self-pity.

God wants to use us and show His favor through us, but He can't do it if we won't let Him and if we won't get out of our own way and allow Him to move. To remember the times, He spoke to us; to remember the scripture He gave us earlier that day, to push forward despite circumstances.

A few days after the surgery, I sat in my bed pondering. The worst part about this whole thing is this catheter. I want to be done with it. Twice a day, two nurses came into my room and transferred me to a recliner chair to prevent bedsores and get my body accustomed to sitting upright again. However, nearly every time the catheter would somehow be pulled on. Every time I moved, its presence would make itself known. Needless to say, it was an incredibly unpleasant sensation. I wanted to go home and in order for that to be a possibility this catheter had to come out.

On Friday afternoon, my wish came true. A nurse name Claire walked in.

"Okay, Sean, are you ready?"

"Yes." I responded

Claire was an older nurse by comparison. In her sixties, she had short silvery hair. It was curled and reminded me of the "typical" grandmother one would see on an old television show. She was kind, but had an edginess to her. I could sense, this was not the nurse I would want to irritate. It appeared she may not be the gentlest either, which, considering the circumstances, concerned me.

"Well, let's get this catheter out." she said.

Great. Just the person I want to be messin' around down there. A sixty-year-old woman, yeah, that's just the vision I had for this. Before I could finish my thought, it was done. Breath immediately drawn out from my lungs, I gasped in total shock. It was certainly painful, but happened so quickly, I can only describe the feeling as relief as it was done and the pain was gone.

Claire left the room and for the first time in a week I started to feel normal. The afternoon passed by and I hadn't urinated on my own yet. Obviously concerned, the nurses began to check back hourly on my progress or lack thereof. By 9 p.m., the call had come from upstairs to put the catheter back in. The nurse relayed the information and said if I couldn't go in the next ten minutes, he'd have no other choice but to reinsert the catheter.

With the seriousness and intensity of a battle hardened soldier I declared, "I will pee!"

I began to pray. Certainly not the most glamorous of prayers, but I defy anyone faced with a re-catheterization to not pray for pee. It's like Elijah and praying for rain in some form, I contest. With the nurse hovering over me, and one last attempt, I peed. Never in my life have I been so relieved in both senses of the word.

God cares about everything in our lives. Our discomforts, our worries, and our littlest hopes are important to Him. His favor and grace aren't limited to big mountains, but if it's important to you, it's important to Him. Never think your requests are too small or too insignificant. If praying for "Sean to rain" isn't too small or too ridiculous, then I assure you, your prayers are not silly or merely trivial.

God is with you. When you're facing your surgery in the morning, His favor is with you. It is undeserved and unmerited. Sometimes, you have to look for it, but it's there. In the midst of your trial, He is right there saying, just hold on. I've got you in the palm of my hand. Look for it and expect it. Expect God to come through for you. Expect God to move in your life. Expect Him to reveal Himself to you. In the midst of the biggest trial of your life, look for Him because He's right there.

He has gone before you. When you start looking for Him and expecting Him to move on your behalf, favor comes looking for you. Good breaks come looking for you. Provision comes looking for you. And in the midst of trouble you can have peace, knowing He is there, just as He was with me.

CHAPTER 11

Looking for Favor

"YeeHaw!" he blared loudly.

We jolted to the left and quickly back to the right.

"This is going to be a good one." he shouted raising his left hand high above his head clutching his imaginary cowboy hat.

Smiling from ear to ear, I glanced over to see my sister equally as jubilant. This is the best part of my entire day. Well, next to snack time or watching Mickey Mouse cartoons while eating lunch, but regardless it's definitely in the top three, I internally cajoled.

We continued to bounce around with chaotic unpredictability as our driver held fast to his old west narrative.

"Y'all hang on now." he said with a thick imitated southern drawl. "She's about to get real wild."

He seized the steering wheel ever tighter as he adjusted his position reminiscent of an authentic bull rider preparing for the most intense eight seconds of his life. He accelerated sharply and we continued to toss and turn our way down the driveway.

With every peak and trough in the wavelike road, an equally abrupt wallow and shout echoed from our driver above the roar of the engine. As his voice filled the bus, we responded in kind, our ever-increasing elation seemingly occupying the cavernous vehicle.

It was a dilapidated old bus. Built in the 1970's, the ten-passenger school bus looked like it belonged in a junkyard. The wheelchair lift in the back rattled along with a cacophony of other jangles as it limped down the road. It was, by definition, the short bus with every bump and thud exaggerated by its rickety, aged suspension. It's passengers only my sister and I. Thankfully, I wasn't alone. While too young to understand its origins at the time, I certainly appreciate now, avoiding another stark similarity with the short bus infamy.

Nonetheless, we had a great time on our brief haul into school and the antics of our driver only added to the memorable experience. Contrary to his hollers and exclamations, our driver was as different from the bus as he was from the old west character he so aptly portrayed.

Phil was a happy-go-lucky guy. Thirty years old with a slender build, he dressed in faded blue jeans and an old t-shirt. He was closer than just a bus driver to us. He was a family friend, the kind of guy we knew we could call on in time of need and he'd surely be there to help. He had children of his own, close in age to Annie and me and was the pastor of the local church. He possessed a certain charming peculiarity about him; a sense that was not lost on those around him. He was a jokester at heart and that jocular attitude only added to the joy of kindergarten. He had worked on the farm for us for several years and thus had a unique connection to our family.

We eased onto the highway and followed the narrow two-lane road into town. After passing the grain elevators, the post office and bank, we arrived at the school. Pulling into the turnaround, we slowed to a stop a mere thirty feet from the entry doors. The sidewalk sloped gently towards the door. Next to the door, it was only wide enough for the entry itself, but it gradually widened as it approached the asphalt. On either side of the sidewalk was grass. A steep incline bordered on the right, while a small patch of flat grass accented the left side five feet away as we began our exodus.

Phil bounded up from his seat and unfastened the straps securing my chair into place. Once free, I made my way to the back of the bus towards the lift. Once outside the bus, he opened the door, grabbed the control panel and hinged the lift outward. Parallel to the ground, I eased my way onto the lift. I had done this dozens of times. It was not a dangerous activity by any means. In fact, Annie would often run the controls under Phil's supervision. Being a typical younger brother, I never liked that she had complete and total control over me in those moments, but it was something I would have to get used to.

Anxious to meet up with her friends, she bounded off towards class leaving Phil and I to do the dirty work.

"You ready?" he said, awaiting my confirmation to begin lowering the platform from its four-foot height towards the ground.

"Yep!" I said enthusiastically.

"What are you going to do at school today, Sean?" he inquired, filling the time with small talk.

I leaned forward to answer his question and adjust my position, but in doing so I unknowingly pinned the control joystick of my wheelchair forward causing it propel itself full speed ahead. In a flash, my 250-pound wheelchair jolted towards the edge of the platform.

Initially, it bounced off the safety ledge, designed for just an occasion, ideally keeping the wheelchair on the lift.

"Whoa, Sean!" Phil exclaimed

It was too late. With the joystick still pinned forward, the chair was an unstoppable force and remaining negligent of its helpless occupant, shot off the platform. Time stood still as the seriousness of the situation began to sink in. Phil, helpless to alter the course of events, could only watch as gravity ran its course pulling the chair forcefully downward.

CHAPTER 12

Looking for Grace

It's always amazing to me that in times of grave danger; our bodies have built in mechanisms to protect us. We often experience a side of general relatively Einstein himself would be envious of as the speed of the world around us slows. If we're lucky, we can adapt, contorting our bodies to soften the oncoming blow. On the other hand, our bodies may also block out the happenings around us altogether and we're left with only memories of the moments immediately preceding the accident. The latter was my experience. While my body was being jettisoned from the confines of the bus, my mind was, for a brief moment, far away, only to be reunited with my limbs milliseconds later after impacting the ground.

I opened my eyes to see the world turned literally on its side. Lying in the grass, I looked over to see the bus several feet away. After further inspection of my surroundings, my chair, a mere eighteen inches away from me also, on its side. Its wheels still turning and casters dangling as the inertia from the fall continued to dissipate. Before another thought passed through my mind, I noticed Phil running towards me, obviously startled and concerned.

"Sean! Are you okay?" he cried out crouching down next to me.

I was understandably shaken, but otherwise unscathed.

"Yeah, I think so." I replied.

"What happened?"

"I don't know." I fibbed.

Worrisome of indignation I decided hiding the truth was the best course of action. Not a week earlier, Dad had reminded me to always keep my chair in a low gear when entering and exiting the bus and I couldn't help but think this was my fault. In leaning forward, I inadvertently pushed the joystick of my chair forward with my elbow. Combine that with a higher gear than I had anticipated or been aware of and the unthinkable became reality.

"Well, let's get you back in your chair." he added after taking a moment to comfort me and compose himself.

He tipped the chair back upright, picked me up, and set me down. I fastened my seatbelt and began to make my way to class.

"You're sure you're alright?" he said looking me over once again for any signs of trauma.

"Yeah, I'm good."

Anxious to tell my buddies about my daring feat, I rolled off toward the classroom.

As I moved down the hallway I couldn't shake the feeling there was more to this occurrence than what meets the eye. Most prominently, I couldn't delineate how I had landed on the grass out of my wheelchair. I always wore my seatbelt; religiously. It was one rule I never broke and yet somehow it was unfastened. Somehow, I landed unattached to that two hundred and fifty-pound hunk of metal. Somehow, I didn't have so much as a scratch on me. I had a sore knee, but all things considered I was unharmed.

The chair should've crushed me. Immediately after leaving the rigidity of the lift platform, it should have nosedived on top of me, pinning me between the concrete and its frame. With the way I sit in my chair, my face would've been the first thing to impact the ground. The cushion between concrete and steel should've been my forehead. I should've broken bones, I should've had scrapes and bruises, and I should've been severely injured, or even killed. And yet, here I was, "walking" away.

I knew that God protects us and that He looks out for our safety and our success, but I never thought about it and applied it to my own life. I'd always heard stories about the people who were delayed to work because their car wouldn't start and missed the fatal accident on the freeway; or stories of young children, who, after getting separated from their parents, are rescued by the "Good Samaritan" stranger; who, after reuniting the child with their parents, is never heard from again. I never imagined I'd be a part of such a demonstration of grace.

We don't often think about it, but protection is a form of favor. It's a form of blessing. Typically, when we think of those words we think of "big ticket" items that make a difference in our lives. A loving spouse, a well-paying job, sweet and well behaved children, but why do we neglect the little things? Why aren't we looking for His favor in every area of our lives?

Often we won't see what we aren't looking for. We question God's provision and hand in our life, but are we looking for Him? Are we seeking His provision? Are we longing for His protection? When we do, it changes everything.

As I look back on that day, it's evident God had given His angels charge over me. He was protecting me and showing me favor before I knew I needed or even wanted it. His love and grace have so many facets that we often don't recognize it as such.

What if I told you that today, someone you see will give you a check for a million dollars, but there's a catch. Of course there is. You'll only get it if you have the boldness to ask. Next to being immensely excited, you'd be on the lookout. You'd have your head on a swivel like a defensive back in football. You'd be looking, waiting, expecting something to change, someone to move, and when you saw it, you wouldn't hesitate to act, because the reward is great.

In the same way, look for what Jesus is doing in your midst. Be like a heat seeking missile, locked onto your target. Be looking for favor. Be looking for grace. Be looking for provision and just watch the indescribable blessings you will experience.

CHAPTER 13

Setback to Set Up

"What if I would've given up?" I asked from the raised platform.

Pausing I looked out upon the blackness. Beyond the edge of that seeming black, and on the other side of the spotlights tracking my every move sat three thousand high school students, parents, and teachers.

Pausing for dramatic effect, I moved down to stage right, creating a more intimate setting. One that seemingly created a one on one encounter with each captivated onlooker.

"What if…" I continue, "I would've called it quits? Said it was all hopeless and basically gave up on life?"

I had just finished showing a short video enabling one to get a glimpse into my life. A glimpse I could never adequately portray within the confines of a twenty-minute speech. It was filmed at the age of seven, highlighting the struggles, the difficulties, but also the apparent determination my family so unabashedly demonstrated.

It was a sap piece done for the Muscular Dystrophy Association, a video designed to foster donations and garner the attention of otherwise indifferent viewers, and it did just that. It sucked you in, grabbed your attention and over the course of three and a half minutes took you on a life journey, but left you wanting more. It left you hungry to see how that tenacious attitude translated into a life of victory and success.

While originally done for an organization responsible for raising awareness and ultimately eliciting donations and this was undoubtedly a very different audience, the effect of the video was still the same. In this setting, it wasn't meant to produce sadness, grief, or worse yet pity, but rather, to bring viewers to a place where they could receive this vital truth I was about to share with them; a truth that, if allowed to run its course, could alter the trajectory of their lives.

"Think of all the things I would've missed."

I let the words sink in and take their full effect as viewers pondered in their own minds what those things might be.

"Just this past year alone, if I would've given up way back then, I wouldn't have had this wonderful experience, I wouldn't have met many of you, I wouldn't have experienced all the fun and joy, and I certainly wouldn't be standing before you today."

Needless to say, I wasn't standing, but taking the time to explain the idiom of "standing" as a figure of speech was a rabbit trail I had neither the time nor the inclination to explore. It would've only detracted from my message.

This was the Eightieth Annual Washington State FFA convention, and tonight was the pinnacle of my year of service. The FFA, formerly Future Farmers of America, is the largest student led organization in the world. It boasts over six hundred thousand members and strives to promote premier leadership, personal growth, and career success. Simply put, it's a youth leadership organization, but to me, it was much more than that.

Through this organization, I was able to compete at an equal level with *all* of my peers. A severely competitive person by nature, I had very few outlets to demonstrate that competitiveness. Sports certainly weren't an option and being the best at video games amongst my closest friends was, as one can imagine, only minimally gratifying.

In the FFA though, I was only limited by my own mind. Competing in speaking competitions, parliamentary procedure, land judging contests, it was all free for the taking, and I jumped at the opportunity to participate.

At the highest peak of the organization, at the state level, is a team of six newly graduated students, elected from amongst their peers based on leadership, teamwork, tenacity, grit, passion, and a slew of other checklist characteristics. Nearly a year ago, I had been chosen as one of those six members, and now at the end of my term, was the opportunity to present an inspirational oration to all those in attendance.

"That's the one thing we need to teach ourselves." I continued. "Even when everything seems dark there will always be light; there is always hope, and there is always a way."

I was nearing the end of my speech. Pausing, I moved slowly to the other side of the stage. Glancing through the bright onslaught of stage lighting focused on me, I could make out a faint figure seated in the front section. The face was a familiar one to me and the sight of her brought a smile to my face.

It was Jodi Monroe. Her eyes were watery and filled with tears. They weren't tears of pure sadness, however, they were a curious mix of pride and slight despondency. She was my biggest supporter over the preceding year. In fact, my year of service would have been impossible if it wasn't for her and her willingness to help.

My post as an officer would require travelling to all corners of the state, and several trips to other areas of the country. I couldn't do it myself; I needed help; physical assistance and caregiving to make this dream a reality. Jodi stepped in without hesitation. Having been a caregiver years before, she knew what it required, knew that it wasn't the most pleasant of activities; yet, without a second thought, was willing to step in and serve me in that capacity. She was willing to make untold sacrifices to enable a young man she'd never met, to experience the fullness this organization had to offer.

Jodi was a slender, muscular woman whose looks mirrored those of Sarah Palin. Her long, black hair tied up behind her head mixed with her skirt or pantsuit made her a near doppelganger at first glance. Upon further inspection, her confidence and impeccable retort of "Oh you betcha!" only added to the similarities. Parallels that in her good nature only added to her appeal.

She was a charismatic woman with a magnetic personality and carried an optimistic attitude and joy about her wherever she went. It was a mantle upon which her charm so effortlessly emanated from her, and the lens through which she viewed the world. She was intelligent, capable, and a seasoned business woman in her own right. She was strong. Physically stronger than many of her male counterparts and embodied what it meant to be a strong independent woman, both internally and in physicality.

Jodi was a devout Catholic and had a passion for CrossFit. She pushed herself to the pinnacle in everything she did. The mother to three wonderful children and second best or mediocrity were not options in her heart and mind.

As I peered in her direction, I couldn't help but remark internally that this moment was made a reality because of her. She had lifted me up, elevated me to a place of prominence, and while her support went unseen by most, it was her backing that enabled me to encourage others, just as I was on this day. She was content to be in the background; to be the unseen pillars in my foundation, taking great pride in my exhortations of others.

Years later, Jodi would be diagnosed with breast cancer. Unexpectedly and out of nowhere, she found herself in the fight of her life; yet without missing a beat, that same optimism and joy carried her through an ocean of tumult, beating the cancer that so abruptly had stricken her. In these moments, she was my inspiration. Never quitting, never ceasing, never letting doubt or uncertainties get her down. We were cut from the same cloth in many ways; and I hoped when the real storms of life hit, I could face them with at least a small portion of the courage she did.

Awakened from my daydream by my own words I persisted. "That's the one thing we need to teach ourselves, that even when everything seems dark, there will always be light. There is always hope and there is always a way."

As I looked out upon the sea of faces, I couldn't help, but hope they would experience the same freedom that I've learned to accept. The hope that Jesus has revealed and refined in me, the trust He was building and continues to build.

I wish I could've sat down with each one of them for five minutes to encourage them, to build them up, to help them understand the call on their life. The call to refuse to be defined by their circumstances and rather than letting this life harden them and find themselves calloused, to rather be refined by it. Not hardened to anger, but molded and shaped into the creation God so wonderfully envisions.

"Even when life's storms hit you hard, even when there seems to be no hope, even when you don't have a friend in the world, there will always be hope."

As my speech drew to a close I couldn't help but reflect on the simplicity of the two most important ways in which God's grace has enabled me to refuse to be defined by my disability, encouraging and motivating others, and also through humor.

CHAPTER 14

The Power of a Laugh

Do you ever crack yourself up? I mean genuinely, have a moment where you make yourself laugh? I do, especially when it comes to a person's tendency to stare at me. As you know, I've never viewed myself as "different" and often forget I'm in a wheelchair altogether. In fact, at times, I find myself observant of other people's stares or hesitancy, thinking "Good grief people, it's not like I have a disease or something!" Oh… wait, well I guess I do.

My life has provided me with its fair share of awkward situations. I learned early on in that making light of those situations is not only easier on everyone around you, but it's a whole lot more fun for you too. Humor is a powerful weapon; and during my teenage years, it found me quite often, not coincidentally as a result of my wheelchair.

Growing up in a rural area, activities were limited. Friday night had a tendency to be dull, but we found ways to make the most of it and thanks to me, even the most mundane activity could unexpectedly take a turn to Awkward Ville.

It was the newest Pirates of the Caribbean movie and we were looking forward to another adventure. We all piled into the car and were off to enjoy the evening. An hour's drive later, we arrived at the theater. Anxious to find our seats, we purchased our tickets and proceeded to theater number eight.

We were early, but being a new movie, a good crowd was already assembled in their seats. In most theaters, the wheelchair seating is located at the very bottom. Front and center and close enough to require constant head turning as you track objects across the screen. If you're anything like me, sitting this close is only a recipe for disaster. Either motion sickness or sleepiness is soon to follow, neither of which are good options, especially when you're already fighting "the wheelchair persona."

No problem! My friends are brawny and strong. They'll just carry me up the stairs, hobble across the aisle, and plop me down in the optimal viewing location. Seems simple enough. I'm sure nothing could go wrong. There are twenty-five onlookers, but everyone appreciates a good pre-show, so let's do it!

Without hesitation, Miles crouched on one side of me with Garret on the other. Cradling me as if my body were a lawn chair, they ascended the staircase.

Carrying an adult in any fashion is no easy task, but to make matters worse, I have very little neck control once I leave a standard sitting position. As we progressed upward, I was left with no choice other than looking straight towards the ceiling; and with no viable recourse, I could only imagine the scene we were creating.

We continued our ascent, and my thoughts were preoccupied with visions of them dropping me like a worthless sack of potatoes, when my shoes began to slip from my feet. Why did I decide to wear these wretched flip flops? I lamented as we took the staircase, one arduous step after another.

Thankfully, I had moral support as I wasn't the only one to lose my shoes. Distracted by their now bare feet on the very public, very much in need of disinfectant surface, Miles and Garret lost their focus. Distracted by what they described as "goo." In reality just some Dots or Mike and Ikes, an onlooker was the victim of unfortunate "cripple kick" to the head. Laughter ensued as this siege on the movie theater summit was quickly taking a turn for the worse.

To add another layer of humiliation to the scene, my pants began to inch southward. They were falling down and there was absolutely nothing I could do about it. Needless to say, I would've been a welcomed addition to Washington's finest plumber convention. In fact, they would've crowned me, "Least Modest Crack," but I digress.

Arriving at our seats, I was understandably embarrassed. The glare of onlookers seemed to stare gaping holes through my head.

But now we needed food. We hadn't eaten in several hours and in typical teenage boy fashion we reverted to caveman days with retorts of "Me hungry. Food now. Me go get!"

Finally at the summit, we couldn't and wouldn't carry me back down the stairs, so we opted for the next best thing. I would stay and save our seats (not like I can defend them anyway) and they would all make their way to the lobby to find some grub.

As they left, I found myself still the center of attention. Faces upon faces focused on me as if blindness isn't mutually exclusive with lameness. As such, I had no choice but to break the silence with a snide remark.

Mustering up the sternest, most sincere expression I could manage I gazed into the eyes of the starry-eyed movie goers and informed them of the real truth.

"What you don't know, is that my friends have no idea that I can really walk." I said pausing.

I looked both ways as if to confirm they weren't within earshot. Content they had caught the meaning behind my sudden intermission, I continued softly.

"Personally, I just find it more convenient to let them carry me. In all honesty, I'm just too lazy to walk up the stairs. Plus, I like the attention."

I leaned back and smiled contently. Crossing my arms as if having told the story hundreds of times.

There unwitting faces filled with a mix of shock, amusement, and bewilderment.

"Hmmm."

They offered as they turned around, eyes wide open and likely afraid of wheelchair boy's next retort.

In truth, that last part isn't accurate. I didn't say anything. Instead, I sat awkwardly basking in the laser beams that continued to lock onto me. Today, I would say it if the situation presented itself, but unlike my height, my quick wit has developed nicely over the years.

It should go without saying, but I can't really walk either. It isn't a ploy for attention or due to a lack of effort. I'm very grateful for the help and support I receive from friends and family, but where is the fun in being the victim of an endless array of stares if you can't make the most of it. Humor is the most powerful of all weapons and I'll use it every chance I get.

Even if it's just in our thought life, we can shift our paradigm, putting people at ease, merely by altering the trajectory of our thoughts. Shifting from a mindset of introversion and insecurity to one of humor and laughter becomes seamless. Making a memory becomes the result as opposed to anger and bitterness.

In that moment, I made a choice. I chose to sit there in uncomfortable silence. While I managed to keep myself from diving into the depths of self-pity, I certainly didn't make the most of it. If this mindset had been a real truth to me, I would've laughed and waited with great anticipation to share my experience with my friends upon their return. As much as I wanted to poke out every single one of those beady little eye balls staring me down, I didn't. It would've been so easy to revert back to the "why me" mentality and dwell on the uncomfortable aspects of my situation; but instead, if we can look for the silver lining, it can make all the difference.

CHAPTER 15

Your Cross

Jesus commands us, "If anyone would come after me, let him deny himself and take up his cross and follow me." (Matt. 16:24). My cross is obvious. A large, overbearing, hunk of metal with wheels makes its presence known without much deciphering. Picking up that proverbial cross every day is another story altogether.

What is your cross? You may struggle with insecurity, battle with addictions, or come from a broken home. You may have been abused; feel as though you've never been loved or perhaps, someone treated you poorly and left you rejected and abandoned. Whatever it may be, He is asking us to deny ourselves. To lay down our own hurts, our own wants, our own desires and to pick up our cross and bear it for His sake; to put it on our shoulder and watch what He will do.

What does that look like? For me, it's often making others laugh, just like in the movie theater. It's bringing humor to a situation at my own expense. It's putting on a smile every day. It's letting the joy of the Lord be my strength and longing for Him to shine through me in every situation. It's hoping and praying that in every dealing, relationship, or communication; others would not interact with me, but rather with Jesus in me.

Secondly, it's using the platform I've been given to encourage others. It's taking the cross I've been entrusted with and bearing it with pride and honor, running the race set before me. It's taking the shaping and molding of this life in stride, growing bolder and stronger with each step.

For you, maybe it's as simple as getting the kids out the door every morning dressed, bathed, fed, and ready for the day. It could be not living the "typical" college party life and instead pouring yourself into your studies and showing Jesus' love to those on your dorm floor. It could be going to work at a job you can't stand, working hard, and doing it unto the Lord. It could even be laying down your plans, your independence, or the ideas you had for your future and doing what Jesus asks you to do.

There's an opportunity for us all to either pick up our cross or walk on by. To struggle and bear it or watch as others do. In all likelihood, it's the last thing you'll want to do. You'd do anything else. You'd go around either side, you'd go under, you'd go over, but you won't want to pick it up and go directly through what God has put front of you.

It isn't easy. I have days where I wake up and don't want to go to work or have a good attitude because my arms feel weak and tired. I get frustrated because I can't put own my own shirt or take a shower independently. I have days where I'm upset and irritated and find myself wallowing once again through the desert plains of "Why me."

I eventually find my way out though. I give it to Him. In picking up our cross, we surrender. We surrender all our wants and desires, our hurts, our inadequacies, and say, "I trust you." I trust you to make me whole again. See, we all have disabilities in our lives; those things that have the potential to bring us down, the darkest parts of our story, those things that we're afraid to let anyone see. That's what God wants to use. He wants to turn that disability into something than brings glory to His name. He wants to turn it into a beacon of hope, a flash of light that gives others hope for their future. He wants to take what was meant for harm; what had the potential to destroy us and use it to promote us; to elevate us, to show us and those around us His glory and love.

Take a moment to reflect on the imagery of the cross. Here's a device that was used to crucify Jesus, a gruesome methodology for murder. And yet, when we see and think of it, what comes to mind? What do we see on top of almost every church in America? We see hope. We see love. We see salvation, restoration, and victory. Just as God turned the symbol of the cross into something good, He wants to do the same thing in your life. He wants to take the deepest, darkest parts of your story and turn them into a shining light reflective of His grace and mercy.

Before Jesus' cross was turned into that symbol, He had to carry it to Calvary. He had to physically put it on His shoulder and do the back breaking work of carrying it to the place where everything would change. That's what He's asking us to do. To put that burden on our shoulders and carry it to where He can change it. To where His love can pour out over us and transform our lives.

The journey may be laborious and treacherous. You may drop to your knees, seemingly unable to take another step. You may fall, drop your cross and struggle to pick it back up, but don't quit walking. Don't quit moving forward because at the end lies victory and joy. Unspeakable joy as God uses your "disability," and your burden to make an impact and bring hope to the lives of others. That's where true fulfillment comes from. Knowing that you have run your race and the same power that raised Jesus from the grave is active and moving in your life. Evidenced by victory only experienced because you picked up your cross.

CHAPTER 16

Capable, But Not Able

The sun was starting to drop lower in the sky. We turned around into a cloud of dust. The wind was gently blowing and as the cloud of dirt and chaff passed over us, it revealed the last piece of wheat to cut for the year. It was triangular in shape and approximately half an acre in size. All the trucks had returned to the field and were parked alongside the road awaiting the finish and the final load to haul to the grain elevator.

As we approached the corner to continue cutting, Dad brought the combine to a stop. He reached over disengaged the header and separator, and throttled the engine down to an idle.

"Well," he said, "you want to finish it, Sean?"

"Absolutely!" I replied enthusiastically.

Dad would let me operate the machine at times, but more often, we were in such a push to finish the field or the piece that it didn't happen. I was more than capable of doing it, and under any other circumstances would be driving a combine of my own while we harvested together. It saddened me as I thought about what it would be like.

It was always my dream to farm just like my dad. How much I would love to drive right behind him, cutting wheat, just off his right flank. I could see it in my mind's eye; His combine thirty yards in front of me, spewing chaff and straw out the back in a whirlwind of dust and pulverized organic matter. He'd loop the corner in front of me, circling around until he was coming back into the cut. We'd wave at one another and smile. It'd be in that moment; I'd know I made it. I had come into my own and now was walking in the footsteps of my father and grandfather before him.

Unfortunately, that would never be a reality. While agriculture is an integral part of society, we all have to eat after all; the operation of large farm equipment is inherently dangerous. They've come a long way, but the risk of fire in particular is still quite high. Almost every year, we'd hear a story of a farmer just down the road or a couple hills over having a severe breakdown resulting in a field fire.

Most of the time there were no fatalities, but often in its wake was a charred pile of remains where the shiny red combine once stood. With such risk, I obviously couldn't run this machine on a regular basis. I'd have no way to get out in an emergency and without quick thinking intervention I'd share the same fate as the charred machine.

Fortunately, this was a controlled environment, or relatively controlled. A flat, triangular shaped piece left to harvest with multiple people standing by, who, if needed, could rush in to get me out.

Dad picked me up and set me in the operator seat. This wasn't a first for me as I had helped move the combine to another part of the field numerous times when we were shorthanded, while Dad followed in a pick-up or grain truck.

"Okay, bud, it's all yours. Finish 'er up," he said.

He closed the door, climbed down the ladder, and walked towards grandpa's pickup. I engaged the separator, waited a couple seconds for it to fully start before engaging the header. The combine growled as all the moving parts began to function in harmonious synchronization. I slowly edged the throttle forwarded to maximum RPM and pushed the hydrostat forward causing the combine to inch ahead.

I lowered the header and continued pushing the hydrostat forward until I had reached a speed of two miles per hour. It doesn't seem like much, but when you have a thirty-foot header in front of you, a complex mix of moving parts, and you're twelve years old, it's fast enough. I continued forward filling the entire width of header with uncut wheat. I had watched Dad do this thousands of times; and now, doing it on my own, I felt like I was king of the world. This was my destiny, this farm, this moment, this is what I was meant to do.

Beaming from ear to ear, I reached the end of the patch, raised the header, pushed the hydrostat forward to increase speed, and began my turn. After making the one hundred and eighty degree turn, I slowed back down, filled the header once again, and drove back the way I had originally come. Off to my right, I could see my dad and grandpa both looking on with approval and intrigue.

Grandpa was seated in his pickup. He wore a short sleeve, light weight flannel shirt. His McGregor Spray company hat pulled down low covering his brow. He often wore a scowl on his face. The kind of expression you'd expect to see from a patriarchal protector with a modest proclivity to worrying. Underneath the hard veneered stoicism, however, there was a loving, caring man who'd do anything for his family. His passion and goal in life simply to leave this world a better place for his children and grandchildren.

I neared the end of the patch. Fifty feet away from Grandpa's pickup, I pulled the hydrostat back until the combine slowly came to a stop. I continued to pull as the machine lurked backward, simultaneously turning the steering wheel to position the header in front of the wheat again. Moving forward now, parallel to my bystanders, I waved, smiled, and continued until I lost sight of them.

Was this as close to reality as I'd ever get? Yes, I am "operating" this machine independently and I was appreciative of the opportunity to take part in my passion and get a taste of what could be, but at the same time it felt cheap. It felt fake, disingenuous at best. The pride and feelings of my father and grandfather were as deep and as genuine as they get, but as far as making a real contribution to the operational efficiency of the farm, is this as close as I would ever experience? For how many other things in my life would that also be the case?

CHAPTER 17

I Can't Make It Happen

Being a boy, and a mechanically minded one at that, I had a need for speed. I wanted to drive and operate anything with a motor and four wheels. I could see it now; windows down on a warm sunny afternoon. I'd cruise down the highway with my favorite country song blasting on the radio and a beautiful woman riding shotgun. I awaited that day with such vaunted anticipation. And yet, how could that possibly be a reality? Firstly, would there be a woman out there who would fall in love with me? Would anyone really want to take on the challenges that I face on a daily basis? And if they did, would I even be attracted to her or would I just be taking whatever came along because it was my only option?

Well, let's cross that "imaginary" fairy bridge when we find the skeleton key to the unicorn stables, I thought.

On another level, how would I even drive a car? Yes, I can drive a combine at two miles per hour, but it's all hand-controlled. How would I drive a vehicle at sixty miles per hour down the highway when I can't even push the pedals? My dad was lifting me in and out of the combine, but how could I get in and out of a car on my own?

I didn't know the specifics at the time, but I knew there was a way for me to drive. Friends of mine in wheelchairs with less strength than I had were independent operators of their cars, and if they could do it, surely I could too. They'd drive anywhere without even a second thought, but I couldn't fathom such a world.

There are a variety of hand controls on the market for disabled consumers. They range from simple and rudimentary levers with rods extending to the gas and brake pedals to high tech computer based systems; driving aids that allow safe and efficient operation controlled by servos, touchscreens, and joysticks. I would need the latter. A vehicle equipped with controls that took next to no physical strength to operate. To add to it, this vehicle would have to be outfitted with a ramp to allow my chair to enter, pull into the "slot" where the driver seat would normally be and proceed to drive.

It was possible, but expensive; ridiculously expensive. Even as intelligent, cunning, and inventive as farmers are, such an outfitting would have to be done professionally. A one hundred and fifty-thousand-dollar expense was not an unrealistic estimate. Are you kidding me? One hundred and fifty thousand dollars. How could that possibly happen?

Contrary to popular belief, farmers are not inherently wealthy. Granted if the price of wheat suddenly jumps to twenty-five dollars per bushel, I would gladly revise my statement, but seven dollars per bushel on a good year is not going to facilitate a purchase equivalent to that of the newest Tesla. I obviously couldn't afford a vehicle on my own either. In fact, even the thought of trying to save up that kind of money made counting the grains of sand in an hourglass seem like a riveting and worthwhile activity.

In my mind; my finite, puny, human brain, it was impossible. Granted, my mantra defiantly declares any-thing is possible, and I would never quit, but I didn't see a logical way for driving to become a reality. There are certain state and federal aid programs that will provide assistance for individuals with disabilities at times, but as with almost any government run enterprise, they're slow, inefficient, and the results are highly uncertain.

I would need to drive at some point. I'd need to be independent to go to college, to hold a job someday, to take a girl on a date, to drive to family functions, to pick up my kids from school. It was a need. Yes, I wanted to drive, and drive fast, but it wasn't just a desire. It was a bona fide, genuine need, and I had no recourse. I couldn't work towards it, I couldn't beg and plead with my parents, I couldn't do anything. It was simply out of my control.

I tried to put it out of my mind, to not dwell on it, to just believe what I read in the bible is true. "My God will supply every need of yours according to His riches in glory in Christ Jesus" (Phil. 4:19). And believe it's practical too. Not just applicable to the apostles of the bible, or people in the olden days, but to me and my obvious need. My need, however, wasn't urgent. At twelve years old, I wasn't headed off to college tomorrow, and as is often the case, timing is everything. Certainly, having the plan laid out before me would've been convenient and a welcomed luxury, but typically, life doesn't shake out that way, and what would happen next, I could've never imagined in my wildest dreams.

CHAPTER 18

Tragedy

It was a Thursday morning. The bell rang and the exodus began; students in a stampede making their way to the lunchroom. I never quite understood the hurried excitement that accompanied the trip to lunch. As a senior in high school and thirteen long years of cafeteria food, school lunch was not one of the many things that excited me. Who I am to deprive others of their coveted "cheese dog zombies" though?

"Miles, can you grab my lunch box off the back of my chair?" I requested.

"Sure." He replied as he handed me the orange and grey lunch pail draped over the handle bar of my wheelchair.

"You have film today in Coles' room?"

"Yeah, we've got a big game tomorrow. Better make sure I know what to do on the court." I added with a sly grin.

I obviously wasn't going to be playing, but being the team manager, I made it a point to partake in every team activity just as if I was. I wanted my level of mental preparation to be on par or exceed that of our best players.

Once inside Mr. Coles' room, the team slowly trickled in. We assembled around the big screen in the corner as Coach Coles put on game film from our earlier contest against our next opponent. We ate in relative quiet as we watched and Coles' critiqued with great detail and precision what needed to change for tomorrow's contest.

He was a great man and one who demanded respect. As a senior, thinking back, I could still hear his voice blaring out to my fellow freshmen classmates years earlier.

"The two most important things you ever need to learn in this life are accountability and responsibility." he declared.

We were affectionately known as green-weenies; and until we proved otherwise, we were the recipients of an endless barrage of teasing designed to strengthen us and make us better students and better people. Mr. Coles was the type of man who expected excellence. He held his students and players to a high standard of success; and as such, every ounce of talent and effort was squeezed out of us. He could be harsh at times, but he'd run through a wall for us, and we'd unequivocally do the same for him.

About halfway through our film session, we heard a knock on the door. I turned to look and saw my sister standing in the doorway. Her face was strained and stoic. She forced a small smile and asked for me to come with her. I knew instinctively something was wrong. Why else would my sister come to the high school to talk with me? Her eyes were watery, her voice uneasy and wavering, yet calm. I knew she'd been crying and as we walked in silence to the car, I broke down in a heap of tears as she placed her hand on my shoulder in comfort. I recomposed myself and kept moving. Just keep it together until you get to the car.

She lowered the lift to the ground. I backed my chair onto it and she raised it back up. I backed into the van, she folded up the ramp and closed the doors. I watched as she walked around the car the get in the driver seat.

How had it come to this? Not a month earlier, Grandpa and I were watching basketball together, talking about the prospects of the Cougars and Zags hitting the hardwood for March Madness. We had plans. We had milkshake bets to settle at the local restaurant. We had golf tournaments to watch together. We had drives in the pickup during harvest to look forward to.

He was the patriarch of our family. The man who—in his unwavering, steadfast love, and determination—always stood for what was right. Now, he was gone. He'd never see me graduate. He'd never see me go to college. He wouldn't be there for my sister's wedding that summer. He was just gone.

He was taken too early, I thought angrily, predictably working my way through the stages of grief. He was healthy. Not even eighty years old. He worked out every day, how could it be my grandpa that was gone? If it wasn't for a freak accident; falling and hitting his head while on blood thinning medication, he'd still be here. I'd still be in the classroom watching film like I should be and none of this nonsense would be taking place.

Over the next couple days, extended family members were notified, funeral arrangements were made, and a multitude of reminiscing took place. Ironically, this was just the type of gathering Grandpa would have loved. All his family in one place, at one time, supporting and encouraging one another, being that shoulder to cry on for each other. Isn't that just apropos? So often, it is in the celebration of one's life that the departed would've experienced their greatest joy. Tragic that most of us don't take the time or get the opportunity to experience it this side of heaven.

The church was packed, the overflow room without an open seat or pew. The pastor stood behind the podium perched on the right side of the elevated stage. He was a kind man, in his mid-forties with a unique connection to our family. It was Phil, the same man who had driven our bus day after day years earlier. The ceremony took on a unique flavor as the eulogy came from someone with intimate and detailed knowledge of not only the deceased, but also the family he left behind.

"Jack Neal was a great man."

He began, his voice a bit shaky, but immediately strengthened by the apparent mental preparation he had done for this moment. It was obvious, he wanted this to be special for us all and would hence refuse to let his own grief for the departed infringe upon his ability to so. He began recounting who my grandfather was; his inherent strength, his refusal to accept less than what was right, and his unshakable love for others. He continued to reminisce, describing in great detail how grandpa felt about those closest to him; his wife, his children, and his grandchildren. He did so in such a way, it felt as if Grandpa himself were standing behind the podium exalting the family he was leaving behind.

"Have you seen my grandson, Sean?" he proceeded.

A lump formed in my throat. Just keep it together, I thought. Being the youngest, I was apparently first to be spoken about and was unsure if that was a good thing.

"He's smarter than a whip. He's an incredible speaker. He's done more than I could ever imagine and he blows me away every time I see that smile in spite of the challenges he faces."

The pride in his voice was unmistakable, and while it may not have been Grandpa's exact words, it might as well have been. I knew he was proud of me. So much so, in fact, that on the way to the hospital via ambulance earlier that year, despite his ranging headache and somewhat clouded mental state, went on and on about me and my ability to be an effective orator.

Yet somehow, hearing those words from the pastor was the proverbial straw that broke the camel's back and I lost it. Unable to control my weeping, I conceded defeat. Giving in to my emotions as tears poured down my face. I was relieved as he moved onto my sister and other members of the family. Each one affected in a similar fashion as he took great care in describing and praising the unique talents, abilities, and connections we shared with Grandpa. This was not your standard funeral.

This was more than just a goodbye. This was the passing of the torch. It was now my duty and responsibility to come alongside my father and give whatever help I could to the farm. There was a gaping void in the business that was my father's life and career and I'd have to step up to the plate. To attempt to be that sounding board, Grandpa and Dad provided to one another for so many years.

With the ceremony complete and our goodbyes commenced. Ready or not, life would go on as it always does and we'd be forced with to cope with a way of life foreign to us all.

CHAPTER 19

The Gift I

As I returned to school, hours turned into days and days into weeks, until some resemblance of normal was re-established. I walked in the door after a long day at school to see my parents sitting at the kitchen counter. I could tell Mom had been crying and I could only think, "Oh no, now what?"

"Hey, bud. How was school?" Dad offered.

"Fine." I replied, unsurprisingly concerned as to what else could possibly go wrong. "We play Tekoa-Oakesdale for the district championship on Friday." I said desperately trying to avoid whatever seemingly bad news was headed my way.

"So I talked to Andrea today."

Andrea was my dad's cousin. She had just been out for grandpa's funeral a couple weeks earlier. She and her husband, Erik, have been indescribably successful in business. They have travelled the world, living and working in Paris, Argentina, and the US, the kind of people with hearts of gold, and I was about to uncover just how pure and precious that gold actually was.

"Oh yeah?"

Suddenly, I was feeling a little better about the situation, hopeful that this wasn't bad news.

"What did she have to say?"

"Well, she said that after being here for Grandpa's funeral, she talked to Erik and…"

He paused as if the next words carried and increased weight to them, words that would fundamentally alter my life's trajectory and direction.

"They want to buy you a van."

I froze. I couldn't decide whether Dad had just said what I thought he did or if my brain had impulsively decided now was a good time to attempt to imitate the effects of hallucinogenic mushrooms.

"What?" I blurted out, unable to contain my excitement and disbelief.

"Yes. She said they want to buy you a van. I asked if she was sure. Saying that it was an incredible offer, but it will likely cost close to one hundred and fifty thousand dollars. She just said that they knew. They have talked and want to do it. She said that we know where to go and what you need so to just go do it and send them the details."

"Seriously? That is absolutely incredible." I exclaimed.

I am finally going to be able to drive myself! How awesome is that! The independence, the freedom, I can finally feel like my own person.

"I don't even know what to say. I don't even know how to accept a gift of that magnitude. I am beyond excited, but just wow!" I continued. I struggled to find the right words. Words seemed so inadequate, so cheap, and so ordinary to describe how I felt. Elation mixed with gratitude and solace only begin to scratch the surface.

How did that even happen? How did that even come up? Why would they do that? Why would anyone do that? That's not normal. That's not standard. People don't just give away a hundred and fifty thousand dollar gifts. My thoughts raced. It just doesn't happen. Sure Oprah, Ellen, and the infinitely wealthy give away ridiculous things, but not like this. And never in my wildest dreams would I have imagined, me, a small town kid from Podunk town would be on the receiving end of such unspeakable generosity.

Dad continued to explain the conversation he and Andrea had two weeks earlier. He recounted how she initially inquired as to my ability to drive a vehicle someday and his remarks as to the monumental costs of such an endeavor, never expecting anything to come of it; merely having a friendly conversation amongst family in a time of heartache. My mind wandered to the miraculous nature of what was taking place in front of me. My life would henceforth be forever changed. This roadblock that stood so obdurately in my path was, in the blink of an eye, shattered to pieces.

How often do we find ourselves in need of the one hundred and fifty thousand-dollar miracle in our lives? A broken relationship, an unexpected layoff, a rebellious child, and a situation that has no hope or means for reconciliation. We can't even work towards a resolution. It's too big. It's too overwhelming. It's too dire. And yet, in the midst of it, miracles do happen. God provides for us in unexpected ways. He knows what we need and when we need it. He's never late, but he may wait until what seems like the eleventh hour. Now, here I was, living, breathing proof of that.

The best part is I wasn't even looking for it. It wasn't even on my periphery. I could've never dreamed of such an arrangement, and yet the puzzle pieces were all put together at the right time in just the right order.

That's not to say I don't miss my Grandpa Jack, because I do immensely. Not a day goes by I wouldn't, in a heartbeat, trade my van to have him back with me, but I believe it was the will of God to use a dire situation, one rooted in grief to facilitate blessing in my life. It's what He wants to do in all of us. He wants us to be looking for Him and His blessing always, even in the midst of strife. Rejoicing in the Lord always; in the midst of turmoil, expecting Him to move, expecting Him to do big things.

When we take the limits off and enable God to move in miraculous ways we develop a "what's next" mentality. We recognize and thank Him for the immense blessings He has poured out, the undeserved, unmerited favor, the one hundred and fifty thousand dollar miracles and say, "Wow! Thank you, God. What you did is, in a word, incredible. But I want to know what are you going to do next? Because I know you aren't done with me yet. You have abundance and provision in my future and I can't wait to see all you have in store."

CHAPTER 20

The Set Up

Ring. The phone clamored in my hand.

"Please don't answer." I thought to myself. "I really don't want to talk to you and I can almost guarantee you don't want to talk to me either."

Ring. The phone continued.

"Well, in reality, I do need you to answer."

My internal dialogue persisted.

"I may not want to screw on my smile and cheery disposition, but you answering would be helpful to say the least, Miss..."

I looked down at my call sheet.

"…Cooper. Actually I am looking for Jeremy Cooper, but assuming you are probably working in all likelihood, I'll be chatting the missus. So yes, Miss Cooper, please answer so I can introduce myself and my firm to you."

Silently, I began to sarcastically rehearse what I would say if someone indeed picked up on the other end.

Another ominous ring bellowed across the phone line.

This is great. My twenty-fifth phone dial of the morning and I'll be leaving my twenty-third message on someone's answering machine. Yet, another call that won't count towards my daily requirement of twenty-five quality contacts. What a perfect way to start off the week, my unbridled cynicism filled the room.

"Hello?"

I was abruptly awoken from my mental journey to Scorn Ville and my self-induced pity party.

"Hello, is this Mr.—"

I forgot his name. My mind went blank realizing the voice was a male, not the female I had been expecting.

Half panicked, I looked down again at my call sheet. "Cooper?" I said finding my place again on the list of names and numbers.

"Yes, this is Jeremy."

The voice replied obviously annoyed.

"What do you want?" he indignantly inquired.

"Well, sir, my name is Sean Neal with XYZ Investments. How are you doing this morning?" I offered.

"Fine. Why are you calling me and what do you want?"

"Great question, sir. I'm just calling to introduce myself. I'm not trying to sell you anything or change your religion or anything like that." I said, futilely attempting to infuse some needed humor into the conversation.

"Good, cause I'm not buying and I'm not religious." he spouted before I could even finish my sentence.

You could use some religion I thought to myself.

This is going to be fun. Over the course of an average day, I would talk to over sixty people and dial close to one hundred and fifty phone numbers encountering individuals on varying points of the irritability scale ranging from slightly annoyed to inches shy of pushing grandma's wheelchair off the Grand Canyon overlook, and this guy was off the charts.

"What do you know of XYZ Investments?" I continued, cautious to my phrasing in order to avoid one word responses.

"Not much" he shot back.

Great! Two words. Much better.

"Well, sir, we are a full service investment firm that specializes in helping people save for retirement, plan for their children's education, estate planning, and various other needs."

"Look," he cut me off, "Not all of us are fortunate like you. Most of us have to work our asses off just to make ends meet. We aren't lucky enough to sit in a comfy office and make the big bucks off of other people's hard work. I don't know who you think you are, but don't call me again. Some of us aren't privileged like you."

Without another word, he hung up the phone.

"That went well. I'm glad that being in a wheelchair has designated me as privileged. Apparently being unable to clothe and bathe myself this morning has elevated my social standing." I thought angrily.

"If only you could see me right now, Mr. Cooper. Sitting here in my wheelchair, you might not be so quick to pass judgment on others when I'd give just about anything to be able bodied like you."

My thoughts and internal dialogue were rapidly depreciating in quality.

It wasn't supposed to be like this. Once I came home, it was supposed to be different. Not that I assumed it would be easy. I knew it wouldn't, but I didn't think it was going to be this hard. I didn't think that every morning I would dread waking up and putting on my suit and tie. I didn't think that something as simple as a phone call would morph into an out of this world undertaking, striking fear into me at the very thought of it.

Over a year and a half ago, I had moved down to Phoenix, Arizona with my mom and aunt in order to be trained in the tricks of the trade. It was through this training I was assured I would come out a more competent, prepared, financial advisor with more opportunities for assuming responsibilities over an existing office, or at least taking part in an asset sharing program. Unfortunately, no such offer had been made. I wasn't bitter or upset about it. In fact, I was blessed to be working in an office with a man I respected and admired. He developed a very successful business over the years and was gracious enough to allow me to invade his territory and work out of his conference room.

Jeff Bollinger and his branch administrator, Carol Fleener, are two of the kindest people I've ever met. From the first day I entered the office, I was greeted with open arms and compassionate hearts. They both seemed to possess an innate ability to see behind the outward veneer and into the very heart of people. And as such, they saw right through me. They were supporting and encouraging, just the kind of environment I needed to get started.

Working for this firm had been a dream of mine for so many years. From the moment I enrolled in classes at Washington State University, my goal was to get my degree in finance and start my career at XYZ as a financial advisor. A close family friend had been indescribably successful as an advisor and I knew there was unlimited earning potential. Before graduating college, I accepted their job offer, and knew I'd be starting my home-based study programs later that summer.

Following my passage of the Series 7 and Series 66 exams, it would be time to move. I would have to spend six to nine months, fourteen hundred miles away from home in Arizona. It'd be a wakeup call. It'd be vastly different from anything I'd ever experienced. Needless to say, a sprawling metropolis is an obvious culture shock from the rolling hills and rural minded inland northwest.

These were uncharted waters and I couldn't pinpoint my exact feelings on the trip. In one way, I was beyond excited. Excited to start making money, excited about the potential, excited for a new adventure, and yet on the other hand I was dreading the move all summer. I knew it was coming, but like an appointment scheduled a year in advance, it seemed the day would never come; until it did.

It was August and with harvest in full swing our departure was heavily dependent upon Dad's harvest schedule. As I needed caregiving assistance, my mom and aunt had agreed to move with me and spend the six months away from their homes as well. Dad wouldn't be staying with us, but we hoped he'd be able to make the cross country drive with us.

While not taking it into account at the time, this venture was far outside my mom's comfort zone. Throughout our lives, my dad had been the prototypical leader of the family. When things got tough, he was the solid rock to turn to, the unwavering, steadfast presence upon whom she relied. Now, fourteen hundred miles away, the responsibility would fall disproportionately on her shoulders. This was a family affair. It wasn't just effort on my part that would be expended. It wasn't just my discomfort that would surface, but rather, it would stretch us all in ways we didn't yet realize.

My final examination was scheduled for the morning of August 27. As luck would have it, a break in harvest coincided with that date. We agreed that following my exam, Dad and I would depart from Spokane, while Mom and Aunt Laurie left from home. We'd meet somewhere later that evening at a hotel.

I said my goodbyes to friends, family, and everything I had ever known and departed for the testing center.

I answered the final question of my exam and waited for my result. After what seemed like an eternity, my score displayed on the screen. Eighty-five percent. Good enough. Relief passed over me as the first hurdle was cleared. I exited the testing room, gathered my report sheet and belongings from the storage locker and proceeded to head towards the elevator.

I looked down at my watch. 9:37 a.m. It had taken me only an hour and a half, which allowed Dad and I to get on the road even earlier than we had anticipated.

Once outside, Dad opened the doors of the van and asked, "How'd it go?"

"Good." I said. "I passed so we're good to go."

"Let's rock and roll."

With that, I loaded into my van, strapped in and headed out for the seven hundred-mile journey that lay in front of us for the day.

Leaving the testing center we headed east on interstate ninety. We passed through the panhandle of Idaho and into Montana before stopping for lunch at McDonalds. It had always been a place Dad and I enjoyed going. The food, while not gourmet, was sustaining and almost always satisfying.

For me, it had a certain nostalgia too. Growing up, almost every summer, Dad and I would make a trip to Seattle for the Experimental Aircraft Association Expo. Hundreds of vendors, pilots, and an air show made for a fun couple of days. As a young man, spending time with your dad is always a treasured experience. We'd often find ourselves going through McDonalds after a day of sight-seeing, ordering two packs of chocolate chip cookies, and heading towards the Puget Sound to take in the view while we enjoyed our feast. It may not have been anything remarkable, but it was me and my dad and that was good enough for me.

We ordered our food and of course cookies and we're back on the road in a flash. We had ten hours of driving to do that day, and being only two and a half hours in there was a long way to go. We drove another hundred miles before turning south on interstate fifteen just West of Butte, Montana. We were headed towards Idaho Falls and eventually Salt Lake City. Three hours later, deep into the outermost regions of Idaho, I suddenly felt far away from home. No longer was the landscape familiar, full of green trees or rolling hills of wheat. It was flat, dry, and desolate. Large rock formations jutted up off in the distance. They reminded me of what I used to see on the old Oregon Trail computer game from elementary school. Chimney Rock. I could remember it so clearly.

Those days were so much simpler and a part of me longed for their return. They were so certain, so steady, and so easy compared to what lay in from of me now. Ironically, it was in that moment I felt almost connected to those trav-elers of the Oregon Trail. On my way to a new place with feelings and apprehension not altogether different from what those settlers must've felt. My future was uncertain. I had no idea what to expect, no foresight into what waited around the next bend in the road, and no choice but to just move forward.

Often, the fear of the unknown can be exponentially worse that the experience itself. I hoped that was the case. I hoped these emotions and thoughts filling my mind and my heart were merely over exaggerated projections. And yet, I couldn't help but feel as though I was headed into the lion's den, as though what awaited me over the next several months was something I would've wanted to avoid at all costs. The feeling that I would come to regret this trip, this drive, and this destination persisted in my mind as the miles passed by. I was afraid, but didn't realize the extent to which that fear would be propagated in the following months.

CHAPTER 21

Trapped in Pain

It took mere weeks for words like misery, heartache, pain, and hatred to describe my feelings towards Arizona, and my new job. The training was a mixture of classwork, in field training, and lots and lots of phone calls. Buy, Buy, Buy was a mantra not merely attributed to the likes of CNBC's Jim Cramer, but a daily occurrence for me in the life of what felt like a glorified telemarketer. Even worse than the phone calls was a two-week segment of our training called "Field Foundations."

It would be our responsibility to meet with a veteran financial advisor and go door to door, introducing ourselves on their behalf.

This is going to be terrible. I have always been a people pleaser and I could think of nothing worse than being a door-to-door salesman. Not only is there a negative connotation associated with such a profession, but honestly, who in their right mind wants to meet someone on their doorstep? Let alone, who will spill their entire financial history to some random dude in a wheelchair they just met? To add fuel to the fire, if we didn't get a certain number of contacts within this two-week span, our employment would be unceremoniously terminated. No pressure though, right?

I suited up in my slacks, button down shirt, tie, and suit jacket, aided by my faithful mom and bounded out the door. I had a forty five-minute drive that morning and it seemed to last forever. Every moment, I dreaded the unknown. I pained at the thought of knocking on someone's door to introduce myself. I looked up at my car's thermometer, seventy-six degrees and it's only 7:30 a.m. This is going to be as miserable as I imagined.

A few minutes before 8:00 a.m., I arrived at my host advisor's office. We chatted and exchanged pleasantries before she outlined the neighborhood in which I'd be knocking on doors later that morning.

"Any questions?" she said.

"No, not really. I think I'm ready to go." I responded.

My only real question was how badly do I have to injure myself to get out of this wretched activity.

"Good luck."

She nodded politely and opened the office door allowing me to exit.

I smiled and offered my gratitude for her help before making my way to my car.

Moments later, I arrived at the neighborhood in which I'd be soliciting. There's really no other way to describe what I was doing. I ignored the no soliciting signs, content that if questions roused, I could blame it on being from out of town and hence, proceeded to walk towards my first house.

I rolled up the slopped driveway, snaked my way around a minefield of children's toys strewn about on the sidewalk, and arrived at the front door. I took a deep breath and began to knock.

Nothing.

I waited twenty seconds and knocked again. This time, I was abruptly awakened from my stupor by the intense growling and barking of what I assumed to be large ravenous dog.

Anxious, adrenaline still pumping, I left the front door content I had given my first house it's fair shot. I continued down the street to the adjacent houses in a similar fashion. The following four, however, rendered me unable to access the front door. Either stairs, obstacles on the sidewalk, or terrain too uneven to be passable by my chair prevented me from even attempting to knock.

At this point, the hot Arizona sun was reaching its peak intensity, and the beads of sweat forming on my brow informed me to the likelihood of a drenched suit by day's end.

I approached the next house and pleased that I could approach the door, knocked three times. Shortly after knocking, the inside door lurched upon. The screen door remained closed, and like many screen doors in Phoenix, it was a security door and I couldn't see anything through it. I could vaguely make out the shape of a person standing on the other side, but nothing further. No kind, welcoming eyes, no reassuring smile, just a blank ominous figure.

As I progressed through my introduction and subsequent fact-finding inquiry, I felt as though I was talking to a deaf mute. I might as well have been standing in front of a concrete wall shouting to someone on the other side. I had no facial cues to go off of. No assurance that he was even listening. For all I knew, he could be Darth Vader unsheathing his light saber in preparation to make my wheelchair even more needed.

This was the final straw. I am done. I'm not doing this anymore. I don't care, it's too hard and I hate it. I'm quitting and going home. There's no way I am going to do this the rest of my life. I was homesick. I missed my family, my friends, the comforts of home; and most of all, I missed the joy I used to have. I missed the contentment and delight I used to experience. I couldn't even remember what it was like to be happy. What it was like to even feel emotions

other than dread. It was as if I was in a hypnotic daze, separated from reality.

I was trapped though. I couldn't quit. Too many people and invested too much time and energy into this experience, into my future. Quitting now would not only be
a slap in the face to them, but I had nothing else to turn
to. No other job, no other option. This was my reality and
nothing was going to change that.

Looking for a glimmer of hope, I turned to my bible
and the word of God. I felt abandoned. I tried so hard to
do what I felt was right, what I felt like God was leading
me to do; and yet, I was in despair. Like we so often do,
I had waited until my thoughts and emotions had gotten
the better of me before turning to the Lord for His help
and comfort. Opening my bible that evening, I unknowingly turned to Isaiah, where the verse I found would've
surely caused me to fall to my knees if I had been able to
stand.

> "I will go before you and will level the
> mountains; I will break down gates of
> bronze and cut through bars of iron. I
> will give you hidden treasures, riches
> stored in secret places, so that you may
> know that I am the Lord, the God of
> Israel, who summons you by name."
> (Isa. 45:2–3)

In my moment of weakness where I felt like all was lost, God was telling me He was going to go before me. He was preparing a way for me so that I may come to know who He is in even greater ways. Not only that, but He was using words that were exactly applicable to what I was doing. He was talking about giving me hidden treasures, riches stored in secret places, when everything I was doing related to money and investing.

Additionally, in my current state of mind, a prison so aptly described my feelings. I was enslaved, entrapped, and entombed into a world I never wanted to experience. Breaking down gates of bronze and cutting through bars of iron was the most comforting vision I could imagine. Lastly, this wasn't just a verse for anyone. No, He was stating so that you may know that I am the Lord, the God of Israel who summons *you* by name. It was specific to me, he had a plan for me and my life, to use this pain and heartache for good.

Moments like these are often few and far between in our lives. Yet, when we encounter them, they give us great hope. Whether in the midst of a medical emergency, a family crisis, a lost job, or a bad break in our lives, when it seems like God speaks directly through His word to us, it changes everything. It moves us and shifts our focus from ourselves to Him.

I was encouraged, motivated, and inspired. It gave me the strength to press on, to keep going and not give in to the pressure around me. The weeks passed by, painfully slow at times and before long, I was back home in Washington. I was working locally and I was sure everything was about to change for the better.

Day after day passed by with little to no success, however. Sure, I had meetings with prospects here and there, but this was not going to sustain me. My commission numbers began to slip and I was in real danger of losing my job.

As I continued to dial for dollars as it was so eloquently described, I couldn't help but think, these gates of bronze should be broken through by now. These bars of iron should be cut, shouldn't they? Where are these secret riches I had been promised? I began to resent this job yet again. I began to doubt, and as I did, the downward spiral continued.

Ring... Ring... Ring... Ring... Another call and yet again, no answer. I left another message. This was stupid. I wanted to do anything else, but felt like I couldn't. My parents had given so much to this, there was no way I'd be able to convince them of the merit in another job. Next to the way I felt in Arizona, I had never experienced feeling so trapped in a situation. I hated my life. You'd think that would've come earlier, given my circumstances, but it didn't. I hated waking up in the morning. I didn't want to go on anymore. First, I had all this other stuff to deal with, being in a wheelchair, requiring so much additional care, having almost no independence; but now, I had to spend eight hours and Saturdays doing the one thing I deplored most. I was letting everyone down. I was blowing it. For the first time in my life, I was failing. Success eluded me;

and no matter what anyone said or did, I couldn't continue anymore.

I started applying for jobs, job after job after job and hearing nothing. Desperate and willing to do anything else, I finally convinced my parents to the validity of letting me go back to school. I contacted the admissions office, registered for classes, met with professionals and financial aid personnel as I prepared for a massive shift in my trajectory. Mere days before classes were set to begin, everything changed.

CHAPTER 22

The Heart of the King in the Hand of the Lord

1-5-0-9-3-3-4, I began to dial another number.

Tap, tap, tap.

I looked up to see Jeff standing on the other side of the French doors separating the conference room, my make-shift call box, and the rest of the office. I put the phone down and motioned for him to come in.

"How's it going, Captain?" he inquired cheerfully.

Over the course of the preceding nine months, Captain had become my jovial nickname. In fact, Jeff referred to me as Captain in far more regularity than he ever used my real name. The origin of the nickname is, to this day, foreign to me, but it did foster a sense of camaraderie between us. It was indicative of the way we had to view our jobs, more specifically my job. He had long ago paid his dues and endured the painstaking process of building a clientele. Nonetheless, he, better than anyone else, understood what I was going through and the toll it was taking on me, though not to its fullest extent.

"It's going." I replied "Another day, another dial."

Trying my best to put on a genuine smile.

"You got a minute?"

"Sure."

Jeff was a full, statured man. To the unknowing onlooker, he could certainly be intimidating. He stood like an NFL lineman, reaching six foot two inches in height and offering the appropriate body dimensions to line up in the trenches against opposing defenders. Underneath that stature of a man was a guy from Arkansas who embodied what it meant to be a "Jolly Giant." He had a way with people, a unique ability to connect with them almost instantly on a deeper level. Superficiality was not his game; he wanted to know the real person he was talking to. Whether it was the janitor or the business owner, he was always the same fun loving guy. He was confident, as he had to be in such an occupation, yet he was kind; driven yet relaxed; and always sported a smile. He was the go-to guy for a good joke and often the cheesier the better.

We had met almost a year ago. While in the final stages of my Arizona trip, I was tasked with deciphering where I'd like to build my business. Jeff had been one of the advisors I met with. In that initial meeting, I remember him leaning back in his office chair. Arms crossed with a look of approval on his face. It was as if we'd known each other for years and it was in that initial meeting he'd offered his office space up to me.

It was no small task to invite some unknown, potentially "hot-shot" stockbroker to come share your space and your office, but he was happy to do it and while I didn't know the nature of our visit this morning I trusted him. I assumed it would just be another one of our chats about what to get for lunch that day, considering we both loved to eat.

"How're you doing back here? You hitting your numbers?" he asked with seriousness.

It was out of genuine care as opposed to supervisory instigation. His facial expression provoked the real truth and not the flowery, ever optimistic story I had become so astute at giving.

"I'm alright."

Trying to give the most optimistic version of the real truth.

"I'm trying. I'm calling and leaving lots of messages. Still not loving it, but doing what I have to do."

He paused as if letting those words rest in the air would somehow alter their meaning. Talking another step forward, he closed the glass door behind him, and sat down in the office chair across the conference room table from me.

I backed my chair up away from my desk and approached the table directly across from him. I could tell this wasn't going to be just a quick visit

"Let me ask you something."

He leaned forward, furrowed his brow, and rested his chin between his thumb and forefinger.

"Would it make any difference to you if you were actually making money at this?"

He paused. I was unsure what he actually meant by this comment. I was making next to nothing; and as my numbers slid further, my compensation was sliding with it. So obviously, having some success and making a decent living, even just a portion of the six-figure carrot that was dangled in front of me early on, would help improve morale for the sailors of the SS Seanship.

"Well, yes." I replied skeptically.

"I know you don't like what you're doing, but you have a real talent for it. If you were making a decent living at this, is it something you'd want to continue with?"

"Yeah, definitely."

"I know you're a good guy. You're smart, you care about people and I know you'd take really good care of my clients."

What are you getting at? I wondered. A tinge of excitement began to rise up in me. Was he about to propose what I think he might be?

"Well, I don't know if this will come to fruition or not, but I wanted to tell you in hopes that it would give you some encouragement about the musings taking place behind the scenes," he continued, "I've already talked it over with my wife. I've already presented it to the home office, and if another office of comparable size opens up somewhere in the northwest, I'd like to take it and have you take over my office here."

Advisors don't typically move around. They pick a destination to build their business and they endeavor to become a pillar of that community, a neighbor and a friend to be counted on in a time of need. What Jeff was proposing was not the norm.

CHAPTER 23

The Gift Part II

My jaw dropped. I tried to string words together into a coherent sentence, but as I opened my mouth to speak, nothing came out.

Sensing my apparent inability to comprehend, he added, "This is your home. You can't just get up and move somewhere else, the farm is here, your family is here. On the other hand, I can move and you are an asset to this firm and to this community. My kids are homeschooled, we don't have any real family ties to this area, but you do. I want you to succeed in this and I believe this job description was hand tailored for your skill set. Carol would do anything for you and the two of you would make a great team."

"I don't even know what to say."

I was in shock. What an incredible gesture. What an incredible blessing. Tears filled my eyes.

"I don't know if home office will approve it and I will obviously take some accounts with me. Mostly family and close friends, but you'd have a good twenty-five to thirty-five million asset base to work with. I think you'd be just fine." he concluded.

"Most definitely." I managed to squeak out. "The fact that you would even consider doing such a thing is incredible to me. All I can say is Wow!"

"Alright, Captain. Well, keep fighting the good fight."

He stood. Patted me on the shoulder and walked out closing the door behind him. I couldn't believe what I had just heard; and immediately, my mind began its attempts to trick me. Valiantly testifying that I had misunderstood what he told me.

I was inspired. With newfound hope, I hit the phones harder than ever. I fiendishly dialed number after number believing even if I couldn't hit my numbers, I wasn't going down without a fight. If Jeff was willing to do something so selfless, so altruistic, so indicative of servant hood and the true giving nature of his heart, the least that I could do was give this one more shot; giving everything I had one last time.

More than anything, I was taken aback by the kindness one man could show. I sat amazed at the favor I was being shown. This is the heart of God that most of us never see. We deserve nothing; and yet, He gives us His best. Not our best, but His. It was a rare glimpse into His love, character, and desire to see us all prosper.

I had done nothing to deserve it. In fact, I didn't deserve it at all. I hadn't kept a good attitude. I hadn't given it my best at all times. I hadn't trusted God would provide for me. I had done the exact opposite and meandered down the path of despair and self-pity. And in spite of it all, God showed He still cared. It wasn't based on my actions, my right living, or my talent, but instead the perfection of His love and character.

I was reminded that the heart of the king is in the hand of the Lord as it says in Proverbs 21.1. I was reminded that these were the gates of bronze being cut. These were the bars of iron being broken through. I was witnessing the manifestation of those verses in an unmistakable and powerful way. Favor was being demonstrated to me in a way that I never saw coming, nor could I ever have envisioned.

A month later, I was offered another job, a job with my alma mater. I'd be working in accounting and finance with a focus on analytics. Good benefits, good opportunity for advancement, and working for the university I had adored from a young age. It seemed to be the perfect fit and after much consideration I took it.

One could argue that because this gift Jeff offered never came to fruition that it somehow dulls the effect of what took place; that when rubber meets the road, it never happened, so it really isn't that amazing at all.

While it is true that it never materialized, it did keep me fighting. It did keep me from going back to school and thrust me into another place that I could still be used by Jesus. It revealed the heart of a man, reflective of the heart of God. Like other times in my life, it made me realize that I had missed it. It made me yearn and wish I had fought admirably all along. I'll never know if it would have materialized had I been willing to fight with everything in me from the beginning, but it should show us all that when we give our best despite circumstances, when God does show up, there is no limit to what He can do.

Yet, it also shows, even when we don't give our best, when we don't hold up our end of the bargain, God's grace is still sufficient.

How many times does God have to come through for me before I get it? How many times does He have to beat it into my tiny human brain before I understand and trust him completely? Apparently, the answer is a lot.

"People don't just give away thirty million dollar businesses."

I mused that night as I recounted the day's happenings with my parents.

"People don't just give away one hundred and fifty thousand dollar vehicles!" I continued. "People aren't always cared for in the midst of trials. People aren't always protected and provided for. People aren't always blessed with a loving and caring family. What could possibly be next?"

138

In the midst of it all, I could sense a building of sorts. My life was stair stepping upward with each rung of the ladder being a new way in which I was seeing God provide in my life. This wasn't a flat line story. This wasn't a level-volume orchestra. This was a crescendo. This was accelerating towards a climax. And I knew what would come next in my life would be even greater. This wasn't slowing down. Like an integral approaching its limit, I was accelerating towards my future.

Little did I know, what was to come next would be the most gut wrenching, heart twisting, humbling experience yet. It was time to play my part and prove that I was willing to give it all.

CHAPTER 24

Dreams vs Reality

Have you ever dreamed you've won the lottery? You're imme-diately filled with excitement. Unspeakable joy passes over you, and yet, you hesitate. Thinking slows down. Rational thought returns as you realize the immense improbability that what you're experiencing is real life. This must be a dream. Pondering the implications, you attempt to wake yourself from your perceived slumber.

Holding your breath, splashing water in your face, con-sulting those around you, and attempting to walk through walls; you try it all, but nothing seems amiss. You don't wake up when you run out of oxygen, splashing water does little more than leave you cold and wet, and spoiler alert, transposing yourself through sheetrock and wooden beams is not one of your hidden talents.

Fully convinced of the reality of your situation, you allow the celebration to commence. Fantasizing about all that you will do with your newfound wealth becomes your pride and joy. Have you ever been there?

Deducing that splurging on one of your big ticket items is certainly permissible, you go about planning your dream vacation; a two week trip through Europe, culminating in a New Year's Eve extravaganza in the heart of Roma. What could be better?

You can already taste the wine, smell the salty Mediterranean air, and can sense the complete relaxation that will pass over you. Just as you click the "submit" button on your airfare purchase, you wake up.

"No!" You groan. You ensured you weren't dreaming. You made every effort to verify the validity of your circumstances before accepting it as reality and yet here you are. From the highest of highs to the lowest of lows. What a marvelous journey. You think sarcastically.

I hate dreams like that. For me, it's usually less extravagant than winning the lotto. I seem to find myself gathered around the Christmas tree during the holiday season as we all open our presents. One by one, the members of my family open their packages, adorned with ribbons and bows. Elated and overjoyed with the contents of the gift set before them. After what seems like an eternity, it's finally my turn to open my present.

Wasting no time, I rip open the paper, shredding the delicate ribbons and bows without a second thought. Using my finger as a makeshift knife, I cut the tape that holds the box together. With the intensity and quickness of a fennec fox, the edges of the box covering the contents are splayed open. Grabbing the tissue paper, I begin to pull it away to reveal the precious cargo inside; and just before its identity is made clear, my eyes open to see the white ceiling above me.

What a buzz kill! Dreams are often bizarre. Whether a projection of the innermost desires of our psyche, compounded by the likes of lucid dreaming activists, or simply random meaningless compilations, we are left wanting more, feeling as if we've missed out on what could've been.

The cool thing about dreams is that anything is possible. The cares and troubles of this world are often discarded as we enter a euphoric state. If only this euphoric state could be manifested in the real world. If only our biggest hopes, dreams, and desires could come true.

For me, that was about to become reality, but waking up wouldn't be as simple as just opening my eyes.

CHAPTER 25

A Moment to Remember

She was beautiful. The faint red highlights in her long, black hair glimmered as the sun danced behind her peeking through the gaps in between skyscrapers. Her smile sparkled as she laughed; and while hidden by the oversized aviator sunglasses garnishing her face, her brown eyes offered reflections of the genuine love she so desired deep within her.

Dressed in her Lulu Lemon leggings, sparkling Toms shoes, white blouse, and red gradient scarf; she was a fashionista, in her own right, a fact that was not lost on me. Unbeknownst to her, I genuinely appreciated her attention to detail. She took great pride in her "put together appearance," and simply put, she was exquisite.

More importantly, she made me laugh. She had a certainly quirkiness about her, a quick wit, and a way of always keeping me guessing. Typically, I have a way with words. I can talk my way out of any situation, should the need arise, but Mia had a way of matching my sarcasm and facetiousness punch for punch. She was intelligent and confident. There were numerous layers to the person she was and I relished the challenge of getting to know the real her.

"That is disgusting!" I quipped.

"It's awesome!" she replied enthusiastically. "We have to make our contribution to it."

Through an awkward mix of laughter and repulsion I continued, "I am not touching it."

"Give me your gum."

"Seriously?"

"Yeah, we're at the infamous Seattle Gum Wall. We can't go without leaving some gum behind."

"If you say so."

I sarcastically took the gum out of my mouth and handed it to her. To my surprise, she took it.

"Thank you!" she said flirtatiously, softly kissing me as she made her way to the wall.

This girl is something else. The grin that had been occupying the central region of my face so often lately returned as she smiled and posed for a photo to cement the occasion.

The gum wall in Seattle, Washington is a tourist attraction in the world famous Pikes Place Market. It is the pinnacle of the old town, hippie vibe often given off by Seattleites. While not at the level of "Keep Portland Weird," the wall is iconic. It attracts thousands of visitors annually, all anxious to contribute. We were no different, and while Mia was without question more enthusiastic about it than myself; leaving some saliva-encrusted ABC gum, where it would assuredly feel welcomed by the plethora of other germ exuding specimens covering the alleyway wall, was a must during our overnight trip to the Emerald City.

Hand in hand, we made our way out of the market. Weaving in and out of narrow streets and hallways, we arrived at the corner of 1st and Pike. It was a mere seven blocks from our hotel, which equated to a ten-minute walk through the heart of downtown Seattle. We'd arrived in town earlier that day at 12:30. Famished from an early morning departure from the farm and the hard four-and-a-half-hour drive across the state, we quickly found a place in the market to eat.

We spent the next three hours perusing the market; doing everything touristy that one can do. Watching the fish being thrown, seeing the original Starbucks coffee, and sampling a variety of drinks and morsels. It was a blast, but now, worn out from an early morning and a constant barrage of people everywhere we were ready to relax before heading to the Mariners game that night.

As we walked down the street, my mind wandered. I'd been in Seattle before. I'd seen these sights and sounds, yet somehow, it was different this time. The colors of the day were more vibrant. The sky was a bluer blue. The sun was warmer and more pleasing. The vendors of the market were more intriguing. Everything was brighter, more fulfilling, and ultimately more enjoyable. Why? It was framed by love in its infancy.

With Mia, I was content to just be. Her presence was intoxicating to me. I couldn't get enough of her. I wanted to know what made her tick and what made her the beautiful person she was. It is often said that love is blind and blinding. It couldn't have been truer for me as everything around us faded away. What really mattered was her. If I was with her and her hand was in mine, nothing else mattered. Infatuation or not, I was all in and would be hard pressed to act differently.

I'd dated other women before, but this was different. There was something unique, something special about this moment, about this time, about this girl and I couldn't help but ponder the future.

As I looked over at her, a smile once again spread across my face.

"What?" she asked shyly as she smiled back.

"Nothing." I responded after a short pause. "Just enjoying the view." I offered teasingly.

Before you bail out on me, I realize we were obnoxious. Yes, we were those star-crossed lovers who everyone stares at with disdain, but we didn't care.

Could this be it? Could this really be what I've been waiting for all along? Could the biggest and deepest desire of my heart really be coming to fruition?

Nearly all of us dream of finding that special some-one, it's engrained in us from a very young age, in order to be happy, in order to be content, we need a partner. Hollywood glorifies it; and nearly everywhere we look, it's paramount.

It was no different for me. In fact, it was of even higher importance to me. Often times, there are men who approach relationships and finding a spouse with a cavalier attitude, figuring it'll happen if it'll happen, but have no real preference one way or another.

Not me. It's always been important to me. Being married and having a family of my own has always been a dream. In many ways, it's been the biggest desire of my heart; and in all likelihood, I have romanticized the notion.

I think a lot. Likely, because I have nothing else to do, and as I grew up my thoughts were often occupied with finding my spouse. I questioned how or why a woman would fall in love with me. Here I am in a wheelchair, unable to personify the very things that make men, men. Strength, physical protection, athleticism all escape me and in my mind, diminished my manliness.

As a young boy, I questioned what I really had to offer a potential mate. I struggled with why anyone, let alone a beautiful woman, would want to take on the challenges that make up my everyday life. There are so many things women want, and as I thought need, in order to be happy and fulfilled that I simply can't offer.

I didn't comprehend the value stored up inside of me. In my immaturity, I couldn't understand the worth I could offer in being resilient. The hope I could bring in providing strength of character. The foundation I could foster in being steadfast. I didn't realize that the intestinal fortitude to press on in spite of the storm before you is the real strength to be admired.

In my mind, I couldn't fathom how a woman could even think of me as a potential suitor when her knee jerk reaction is to assume my mental faculties are lacking. I was limited in my vision. I was inaccurate in my perception. Yet, I would refuse to give up.

Now, here I was with Mia by my side, and it was though I had finally made it. I had seen this moment with my eyes of faith; and now, it was here. It was a reality and a part of me still couldn't believe it. It was as if at any moment I would wake up from this dream and be back on the farm with nothing but the proverbial cows to keep me company. But it wasn't a dream, and we don't have cows.

Everything I had done in my life was in some way related to this goal. I worked hard academically and pushed myself in college to earn a quality degree in order to land a job that would enable me to provide. I persevered through those things that were tough and challenging knowing they were shaping my character, refining my heart, and preparing me to be a servant in a relationship. In every situation, I was pursuing integrity and striving to act with honesty and purity. I most certainly failed my fair share of times, but it was a constant fight to be the type of Godly man worthy of the Godly woman I prayed for.

For years, I had questioned my decision as a young college student to end a previous relationship, but now, it was easy to see I had made the right decision. Wasn't it? Countless nights, I had lain awake thinking how I threw away a perfectly good relationship because I felt it wasn't right. I battled in my mind, hoping my fears of not finding anyone else wouldn't be realized. But now, looking back, how could I question my decision? My choice was validated in this woman standing beside me, or so I thought.

CHAPTER 26

My First Love

"Trevor, you want to go divin'?!" I bellowed in excitement.

"Yeah, man! Let's do it!" He responded equally as energetic.

"Awesome, let's go to the deep end. This is gonna be sweet!"

We made our way to the deep end of the local public pool. It was the peak of summer. A hot July day, and there was no place I'd rather be than swimming. I was fifteen. Trevor, three years my junior, and his two sisters made up our group for the day. We often swam together as his elder sister, Heidi, and I were dating one another. That is as much as one can legitimately date at fifteen years old. Nonetheless, she was my first girlfriend and the four of us always had fun.

I subconsciously knew her younger siblings were our companions as a result of parental need for a chaperone; and what better way to offer supervision over two teenagers than by sending along the twelve-year-old younger brother and nine-year-old sister, Katie, right?

Regardless, we made the most of every opportunity together and today was no different.

Now treading water in the deepest part of the pool, I turned and moved within arm's length of Trevor. Just barely keeping my head above water I uttered, "Ready?"

"Ready."

He nodded.

"On the count of the three..." I continued, "one... two...three..."

I took a deep breath and Trevor placed his hands on my shoulders pushing me downward beneath the surface of the water. Once under a mere two feet, he placed his feet on my shoulders, and with all the strength, he could muster pushed me down further yet.

Trevor was a "string bean." He was lean, but athletic. Having his mom's metabolism and his dad's swimming genes, he personified and embodied the prototype swimmer's physique; long arms, slender torso, and big feet. Had he possessed the proclivity to do so, he undoubtedly could've been a very successful competitive swimmer.

He was a comic at heart, always looking for a joke to crack or an adventure to be had. Beneath the metaphorical jester hat, however, was the caring heart of a guy who would do anything for anyone. He'd give you the shirt off his back without a second thought; and while not even in his teens, the seeds of his character were plainly seen to everyone he met.

Trevor and I had a unique relationship. On one hand, he was the little brother of the girl I fancied, but on the other hand, we were best pals. Our age difference was moot and I enjoyed his company. Perhaps on a subconscious level, I felt we were, in some way, connected after running him over in our early years. Yes, I did say run him over... Let me explain.

On a warm spring day in first grade, we had a bubble party. What's a bubble party? Exactly what it sounds like, you make lots and lots of bubbles; riveting, I know. Welcome to small town America in the 1990s. As his older sister was in my class, he often came to different class activities, and it was no different on this day, until it was.

As the party progressed, I looked up to see the biggest bubble I had ever seen. The thing was huge! As I gawked and looked upward, the bubble began to shift; suspended fifteen feet in the air, it moved higher and higher. In order to keep it in my frame of reference, I began to move my chair backwards.

Unbeknownst to me, Trevor was watching that same bubble several feet behind me as my chair continued in reverse with increasing velocity we collided. Abruptly awoken from my bubble stupor, I reversed course and rocketed forward.

To my dismay, out of the corner of my eye, I could see a limp figure being dragged behind my wheelchair as I moved. It plopped and bounded with every uneven plot of sod. Instantly, I stopped and crawled out of my chair to survey the damage. A rush of onlookers converged on Trevor to find his leg wedged between the metal frame and the drive wheel of my chair.

Horrified and overcome with guilt, I felt helpless.

His mother, understandably wrought with fear, sobbed with screams of, "Trevor! My baby!"

After several minutes, which seemed like hours filled with a symphony of my, "I'm sorry Cheri. I'm so sorry!" and her cries of agony, the paramedics arrived to free him.

He was taken to the local clinic, where he returned from his state of shock. To the relief of him, his mother, and certainly me, he was unharmed. Traumatized, but otherwise unharmed. It wasn't nearly as bad as it could've been, and nonetheless, we've had a special bond ever since.

But that was then and this is now. As the force from his downward push faded, my feet gently kissed the bottom. With what little strength I had, I pushed off and upward as I ascended towards the surface. With the drama and perceived elegance of a humpback whale breaching, I shot through the viscous surface with a gasp for air.

"That was awesome dude!"

Invigorated, I said, "Let's do it again!"

"Okay, ready?"

"Ready. One…two…three."

We continued another three or four repetitions before I surfaced to the panicked screams of the lifeguard.

"Trevor Austin! What are you doing?!"

Obviously she was not the most observant lifeguard as we had been following this procedure for the past several minutes, but I understood her concern. From an uninformed onlookers' perspective, it certainly appeared that this twelve-year-old was trying with all his might to drown this poor disabled teen. Not a perception that I relished, but not all that farfetched either.

"Uhhh…" he frantically searched for words.

His face blanketed with the expression I imagine an ostrich having immediately preceding the act of thrusting its head into the sand.

"Trevor. What are you doing?" she clamored a second time.

Trying to explain our actions wasn't that simple. See, unfortunately for me, my body floated. Lack of muscle and increased body fat percentage meant I floated like a life jacket in salt water; and try as I might, I could only get six inches below the surface on a good day. This activity was a blast for me. I loved the water and this methodology for "diving" allowed me complete freedom of movement away from the confines of my chair.

Pausing between each word for increased clarity and emphasis she asked a final time. "Trevor. What. Are. You. Doing?"

"He likes it!" he squeaked, asserting his innocence.

It was true; and while we parted the deep end tails tucked between our legs, this was the meaning of summer. Unable to work on the farm, like I otherwise would have, I spent my days with Heidi and her family. My second family, as it was, and had the time of my life.

Nearly every day was some variation of the same thing; lunch, swimming, relaxing, dinner, and a glimmer of hope that Heidi and I would find some time to ourselves.

While I enjoyed her brother, sister, and family; it was never really about them, nor should it have been. It was about us. I cared deeply for her and had known her all my life. From mommy and me group as a young child, to birthday parties at four years old, and attending school together starting at five, we knew each other about as well as anyone can.

Heidi was the pinnacle of sweetness. She was kind, caring, and athletic. With blonde hair and green eyes, she stood as a five foot four testament to her Swedish heritage. She had an innate ability to love and care for those around her. She was incredibly empathic. She exuded a childlike faith and had this endearing innocence about her. Like me, she was strong in her faith, but as I didn't realize until years later, she had an even better understanding of the Father's love than I did.

Her mantra was to live a life of love. They were the words she lived by, the prism through which she viewed the world. And on top of it all, she was beautiful, the kind of beautiful one possesses when that beauty emanates from the soul.

For years, it had been assumed we'd end up together. My sister often teased and hinted at it, as I attempted to brush it aside. We'd already been in a wedding together and it had the makings of an all American love story.

CHAPTER 27

Fear or Faith

We were six years old. I was the ring bearer and she was the flower girl. Standing in the back of the church, dressed in a rented tuxedo, and a miniaturized bridesmaid dress, she looked over and smiled at me. Her hair pulled back behind the ribbon that perfectly garnished her blonde locks.

"Do you want to hold hands, Sean?" she innocently inquired.

"No. I don't. I have to hold this pillow."

A miserable attempt at an excuse.

"I'll go ask if we can."

Unfazed by my apparent disinterest, she bounded off to find the appropriate party to facilitate her desire.

Musing what other excuses I could muster up, I shook my head hoping for a breakthrough. It wasn't that I didn't like her. She was great, but I was six, and girls were not on my radar. I would've been content to play with tractors in the sand with her for hours, but holding hands... Come on now. My synapses failed to fire at optimum efficiency and before reaching the area of my brain reserved for such an emergency she returned.

"Sean, they said we can hold hands if we want to."

She smiled softly and extended her hand towards mine, her big green eyes staring into the depths of my heart. As she batted her eyelashes, I knew there was no way I could say no. Doing so would most certainly crush her. What kind of guy would I be if I made her upset? There's a special place in hell reserved for people who make little girls cry.

"Okay."

I reluctantly reached out and grasped her hand in mine, content to the fact that I had just been bested. She certainly is persistent, isn't she?

Pleased and satisfied, she turned her gaze forward as we prepared for our journey down the aisle.

It was the kind of love story you read about in books. Something that could only be put together by God, or so we both thought. Now here we are, eleven years later, attending our junior prom together. We had been a together for the past two years, attending two proms, numerous dances, and a variety of other family functions together. I loved her and felt assured of our future together.

I knocked on the door. Tap, tap, tap. Ken, her dad, opened and greeted me with a smile.

"Hey! It's the Seanman! You're looking dapper this evening. Come on in."

"Thanks." I offered.

I pulled through the doorway; and as I peered to the right, I saw her, standing there in this elegant dress, flowing perfectly down towards the floor.

My jaw dropped, "Wow, you look beautiful." I managed to say, the words a poor representation of her true magnificence.

"Thank you" she jabbed with a wink. "You look great too."

That was the moment I thought I knew. She was standing there in that blue dress looking almost angelic. This was the woman I'd spend the rest of my life with; and somehow, she felt the same way about me.

It was perfect wasn't it? We loved each other. We both loved each other's families and it just worked, didn't it? After all, her family loved, accepted, and supported me, which was no small feat either. Here, their seventeen-year-old daughter was seriously dating this disabled young man, intent on marriage. It was a foregone conclusion, in her mind. Did they have reservations? Probably; but none they ever voiced or expressed. They were at peace, content, and willing to support us both in this journey. They didn't question Heidi's maturity in taking on whatever challenges may come as a result of having a husband in a wheelchair. They didn't plead with her or attempt to dissuade us otherwise; rather, they just stood firm, willing, and able to tackle this perceived challenge, just as my parents and I had all these years.

There were so many good and wonderful things about it, yet I wasn't convinced. As the years progressed, I couldn't shake the feeling that it simply wasn't right. I loved her and cared deeply for her, but it seemed like it equated to an "arranged" marriage. It wasn't, but aspects of it certainly paralleled. It was just so easy, but I wasn't all in. She was assured of "us," but because we grew up together, neither of us had to "fight" for it. We didn't have the opportunity to let our feelings develop; it just happened and was there. Before I knew it, marriage was just the logical progression.

I couldn't do it. It wasn't right. There were other things I needed to experience. We were young and immature in many aspects; and by the fall of 2009, I knew it had to end, but how?

It wasn't meant to be, but fear kept me from following my heart. My head was bombarded with thoughts and questions. Fear filled projectiles launched right at the core of my biggest insecurity. If I ended it, would I ever find someone else? I surely hadn't experienced other women beating down my door, so would I end up alone? Was it Heidi or nobody? I wandered through the jungle of my mind for weeks without an answer.

I was praying and seeking the Lord. I cried out saying, "God, I need you to speak to me. I don't see this as what you have for me. I believe you are leading me in another direction, but every fiber of my being quakes with trepidation. I don't want to end up alone. I don't want to give up something that could've been great, and gain nothing in the end."

You know the kind of fear that surrounds the biggest decisions in your life? The kind of fear, where inherently you know, correct or incorrect, the decision you make today will affect your life in a profound way; and years from now, you'll either be filled with gratitude or regret. There's no middle ground. It's black and white. What do you do in those moments?

Sometimes, we never know we can fly until we take the leap of faith and spread our wings. I'd come to the point where being alone no longer scared me, knowing that continuing with her out of fear was not only a disservice to me, but an injustice to her.

Two years later, Heidi was married to someone else and I hadn't gone on more than two or three dates during the same span. A part of me felt regret, like I blew it, and now it was too late. Surely, I didn't hear the Lord correctly. I must've made a mistake.

Yet timing is everything. Years later, I would meet my next companion thinking, "This is it!" "This is what I've waited so long for!" If I would've known it'd be six years between women, would I still have done it? Yes. Would it have been nice to see what was coming all along? Of course. However, if I'd had that foresight ability, there's a good chance I would've avoided what would come next too.

CHAPTER 28

A Dream Come True

I was tired of waiting; six long, arduous years with seemingly no progress. I wasn't desperate, but it was a desire and a longing that with every passing day seemed increasingly likely to go unfulfilled.

I started out so hopeful, so full of faith, and yet, time and again doubt would rear its ugly head. It would shout from the rooftops of the inner sanctum of my mind reminding me of every time I had tried and failed. The constant barrage of uncertainty replayed in my mind like a worn-out soap opera episode. Being reminded after each and every attempt at taking that courageous leap of faith and asking out the cute girl at the park, only to be rejected yet again was all but unbearable.

As we so often do, I had moved from "absolutely it'll happen," to "well, I hope it happens," to "I think it might," and finally to "I don't know if it ever will." The downward spiral had begun its apparent irreversible decent. When we can't control outcomes in our lives, we are at the mercy of our own inner voice, which is often the most cruel and brutal of them all.

It was time to try something different. If you do what you've always done, you'll get what you've always got, so let's think out of the box. Yes, I turned to online dating. eHarmony it was. Awkward at first? Most definitely, but in today's twenty first century, social media-driven world, the success rate is becoming increasingly higher. At least that's what I told myself to rationalize my conversion to the dark side.

After a few months of "searching," and concluding online dating is not much better, if at all than the real world, I matched with Mia Bennett from Fargo, North Dakota; her dynamic smile and big brown eyes drawing me in almost instantly. Sporting a red hoodie and white undershirt, she looked kind, sweet, and endearing as she grasped chopsticks in her hand. Perusing the remainder of her profile she looked fun, full of life, and quirky. She was not your typical, everyday girl, and that intrigued me. She was attractive, half Japanese, even exotic, and in my mind, warranted getting to know better. Time would tell if she felt the same about the small town "white boy."

To my surprise, she did and we instantly hit it off. Three weeks, countless text messages, and numerous phone calls later we were planning our first in person visit.

"Did you watch Happy, Thank you, More Please? It was great, wasn't it? What was your favorite part?" she asked in rapid succession.

"I thought it was good. A bit of a chick flick, but I definitely enjoyed it." I responded.

I couldn't decipher her fascination with this movie. She had insisted I watch it and there was something about it she wanted to share with me so badly.

The film is a self-described story of relationships. It follows the path of several pairs trying to find their way in life. Centered on the tagline, "go get yourself loved," it's certainly a bit cheesy, but one such pair in the movie touched a core with Mia.

"So why did you want me to watch this movie so badly?" I offered.

"You remember Annie and Sam #2?"

"Yeah." I responded trying to decipher where she was going with this.

Annie was one of the main protagonists of the film. She was an Alopecia patient and worked at a non-profit in the heart of New York City. Sam #2 was a coworker. Someone who had an eye for Annie, but one she wouldn't give a chance to for an extended period of the film.

"You remember how Annie never really "saw" Sam #2 for who he was until she let her guard down?"

"Yes." I said instantly knowing the exact scene she was referencing.

In fact, it was the very scene that while watching reminded me so vividly of the way I felt about her. During the scene, Annie who had finally agreed to go on another date with Sam #2 abruptly tries to end any future interaction between the two of them.

Persistent and not easily swayed, Sam #2 insists that Annie hear him out before she leaves. The dialogue goes as follows:

Sam #2: You can hear this, close your eyes

Annie: What?

Sam #2: I just want you to listen to me. Humor me, please?

Sam #2: (Annie closes her eyes) It's not easy to be adored—you in particular— you have a tougher time with it than most, I get that, but I want you to give it a try. Think of it as an experiment. I promise I will be wonderful at adorning you, Annie. It's an area where I think I have a great deal of talent. You're worth adoration, Annie, you're worth it, and the fact that you don't believe it has nothing to do with whether it's true or not. It's true for me, and that is all that matters.

It described in words what I could've never voiced in my own way towards Mia. I couldn't equate it to love; it hadn't been long enough, had it? But I knew how much she meant to me. She, on the other hand, was talking about the other side of the coin. Following this interaction, Annie's perception of Sam #2 radically changes as she awakens to the person and the soul that Sam #2 truly is.

"Well, that's kind of how I see you," she continued, "once I let my guard down, I realized in greater clarity how blessed I am to have met you. I want you to know that I've never "seen" your wheelchair, Sean. It's always just been you, and once I gave myself permission to let my guard down, I realized even more the amazing person you are."

I didn't know how to respond. I was rendered speechless.

For the first time in my life, someone actually saw me; and I don't mean physically, but truly saw the person I am. She looked beyond the wheelchair, beyond the phys-ical weakness, beyond the absence of normal, and peered into my very being. She saw me the way I saw myself; *wheelchairless.*

In her eyes, I was without blemish, without disease, without iniquity. It wasn't that I was perfect or some ideal-ized version of myself, but the true me; the person that if you could strip away the exterior, break aside the facade of illness and impression of the stereotypical wheelchair user, you would see. You would see what she saw, the real Sean.

Whether lack of time, interest, or sheer ignorance; no other woman, outside of my family and close friends, had done so in my life. I'd never felt it, never experienced being seen for whom I really was, and a part of me couldn't believe it was happening. For so long, the forces of this world battled my soul for what I believed and knew to be true, that at some point in my journey, I began to believe the lies. To believe on some level, perhaps, subconsciously, that because I'm different or don't fit the mold of "normal," I somehow didn't deserve the best this life has to offer. But when someone came into my life and saw past that, it shone the brightest of lights upon my heart. It enabled me to become a truer version of myself. It empowered and validated the picture I held in my mind's eye all along.

Mia was that person. It was evidenced in everything she said, the way we interacted with one another and personified the first time we met in person.

CHAPTER 29

Too Good to be True?

Palms sweaty, I sat nervously in the airport terminal. I was plenty early, as I usually am, and had spent the last twenty minutes alternating between checking her flight status on my phone and wondering why it was so out of the ordinary for someone to be waiting at the edge of security with a single pink rose.

It had to rival a blind meerkat looking for his deaf warthog because every passerby stared me down. Some offering retorts of "awe" or sneers of "cute flower," but mostly just an onslaught of stares. I was used to it and was just anxious to meet this girl I had spent hours every night talking to.

"Flight 967 with service from Seattle, Washington has arrived and will be de-boarding at gate A3." The call came over the loud speaker.

That was it. Her flight was here and in just minutes, the moment I'd been waiting for will have finally arrived. I watched the exodus of passengers as they exited security; old and young, overjoyed and wrought with apparent sadness, the various individuals as different in their demeanor and physical stature as they were in their final destinations.

Stupidly, I began to worry. She did know I am in a wheelchair right? I didn't neglect to mention that in our hours of conversations, did I? Surely, she won't come through security and see the guy she's been talking to these last weeks, realize he's in a chair, and just as quickly as she arrived, be on the next flight out back to North Dakota. My mind continued to launch its attack on my senses.

Not wanting to miss the sight of her as she rounded the corner, I moved back and forth trying to find the clearest shot of the entirety of the hallway. As I peered in and around the masses, there she was. Our eyes locked and a soft smile spread across her face. I moved forward towards the line separating the unsecured and secured areas of the terminal. Her pace quickened as her gazed locked onto me.

She had joked about jumping into my lap upon seeing me for the first time, but little did I know her excitement would indeed be so aptly described.

"Finally!" she exclaimed as she dropped her belongings and enveloped me in her embrace.

"So good to see you." I offered.

The words a poor representation of the feelings I really had.

I wrapped my arms around her as she tightened her grip. I had never been embraced in such a way. So often, people are afraid of hurting me or perhaps "catching" whatever illness plagues me that touch is often disregarded. So much is communicated in the simple embrace of another and as we stood there, enraptured by one another, entangled in our first encounter, for the first time in my life I felt desired. I felt longed for, a feeling that while foreign to me, enabled me to fall even harder for this girl.

Over the following months, our relationship only deepened. She would travel to visit me three more times and I would venture to North Dakota to meet her parents as well. We were in near constant contact, truly infatuated with each other. In both of our minds, this was it; our final relationship, the one that we had both waited for.

I thanked God every day for her. Every time I saw her, talked to her, or even just thought about her, I was drawn to giving thanks. I was reminded of God's love for me; that He would send someone so beautiful, so loving, so seemingly perfect for me. She was such a perceived blessing in my life. Whenever we were together nothing else mattered.

During one of our many heart to heart visits, however, she confided in me some intimacies from her childhood of how she experienced abuse at the hand of a trusted family member. We all have baggage; something in our lives that has been challenging and difficult to overcome and my heart ached for her and yearned to wipe away her pain. It was a wound deep within her, which would set the stage for what would come next.

Little did I know, it was that wound that would create a divisive wedge between us. Unhealed scars from the past that while originally appeared to be mended, were gaping bondages I couldn't fix for her. I could only offer my love, support, and encouragement. It simply wouldn't be enough.

CHAPTER 30

To Live is Christ, To Die is Gain

The lights from her car rounded the corner at the bottom of the hill. My pulse quickened, dreading what I knew was now only moments away. How had it come to this? It had started out so great, so seemingly perfect, and she had only moved here six weeks ago. This was supposed to be the beginning not the end.

The crisp October evening air turned a frigid chill as I heard her car pull into the drive way. For the past sixty minutes, I had sat alone on the patio awaiting her arrival. She had coffee plans with a new friend that evening and waiting for her to arrive home only heightened the anticipation in the most unpleasant of ways. The mantra in mind continuing over and over as I listened to my Spotify playlist was, "For me, to live is Christ, to die is gain." The only words that gave me solace in what I knew I had to do.

I didn't want to end it with Mia. I loved her more than anyone I had ever met. I would give my life up for her in a heartbeat. I longed to be a living sacrifice; a living breathing representation of the way Christ loved the church and so gave His life up for it and now He was asking me to lay down my own wants and desires for His purpose, even though I didn't understand it.

How did we get here? To be honest, it's complicated. Early on, Mia had expressed her desire to move out of North Dakota.

"I'm either moving to Washington or somewhere else, but I am not spending another winter in Fargo." she defiantly quipped early on.

I knew she wanted out and I wanted to be with her too. We both longed for the normalcy of a "traditional" relationship. The joys and discomforts of long distance companionship had run their course and by the time August, her month to move, came it was well overdue in both of our minds and hearts. We desired to date like a normal couple; to be able to see each other more than just extended weekend trips and just be, without the pressure of having to make the most of every second we were together.

Upon her initial arrival, it was everything I had hoped it would be. We'd eat dinner together, enjoy the late summer sun, go to church together; finally, we could just enjoy one another. However, it wasn't long before the wounds of her past began to surface. While I can't completely blame it on her past, I believe there is a strong correlation between those unhealed scars and the hurt that began to surface.

At a certain point, we all have to take responsibility for our own actions; and regardless of what transgressions plagued us in the past, we either become softer, more compassionate, more empathetic towards those around us or we harden our hearts. We put up walls designed to keep ourselves from getting hurt again. We default to impenetrable defense mechanisms that while constructed to keep pain away, end up trapping it inside. While sustainable for a time, before long, those pains surface. Often as anger or coldness to those who are closest to us.

In this case, the walls and defense mechanisms took the form of desiring control. Mia wanted to protect herself and in turn those closest to her. An "us against the world" mentality was seeping into the outer edges of her heart. While such a mindset isn't inherently bad, it was pulling me away from the mold that had crafted me for so many years. It was pulling me into her and away from the loving, caring, support offered by my family. A man leaves his mother and father and clings to his wife, as he should, but there was a whole other dimension to this pull; a definitive exclusivity, a certain harshness, even rudeness, and a lashing out if someone got too close or upset her plans to create a universe for the two of us.

As I witnessed these things coming to fruition in this girl I cared so deeply for, I again turned to the Lord for guidance. I sought to find the "magic formula" that would enable ultimate freedom for her and consequently a freer love for us both. Praying one morning on my drive to work, I distinctly heard the voice of the Lord telling me, "Sean, you're in the way."

I don't often hear God in this way, but I've never been one to put Him in a box and I believe if we avail ourselves to Him, He is faithful to show up in times of need.

"No, no, no. That can't be what you're saying to me" I responded.

I understood through the revelation of my heart exactly what He meant, but I wasn't willing to accept it just yet.

He couldn't do what he needed to do in her with me in the picture. She was finding her hope, her security, and her provision in me, something that, at the time, I desired to provide. Being human, as we all are, I will fail her though. Sooner or later, regardless of my efforts and commitment, I will fail to be what she needs and expects me to be.

"Just give me one more chance, God." I pleaded. "Let me try one last time to confront her; and if she will grab hold of this, get counseling and work on some areas in her life, let me be the one to stand by her and support her through it."

I wanted it to work so badly. I loved Mia with everything I had and for so long; I had desired some form of separation from my parents. I'm so grateful for all they've done and provided for, but selfishly, I craved the freedom I'd experience in living separate from them. Here, Mia was a path to that freedom. Together, we'd have privacy and companionship. She'd be a lover, a partner, a helper, and she was willing to do it all with the added bonus of my longing for independence finally being satisfied.

Securing approval, I felt inclined to do just that. My relief was short lived, however, as when I brought up the issue again with her, I was met with the same resistance, anger, and hurt that had been so prominent before. I was heartbroken. I was pained and full of love for a woman I had to say goodbye to, which brings us back to that cool October night.

She walked through the door with that same smile.

"How was coffee?" I asked

"Great! I didn't expect it to go that long, but Rachel and I really hit it off. We just kept chatting and chatting and the next thing I knew it was 8:30."

"That's awesome. I'm really glad to hear it. See, I knew you'd make friends of your own quickly once you got here." I was filled with even more dread, as she was about to be abruptly shaken from the high she was currently experiencing.

"Well you want to grab a blanket and come outside on the patio for a bit? It's super nice out tonight." I said, looking for an area where we could have some privacy.

She picked up a blanket, ran downstairs to put on a sweatshirt, and we headed outside.

Break ups are never fun, but they're even worse, downright impossible when neither party involved desires it.

She sat down in an old wicker lawn chair. With the blanket neatly wrapped around her, I pulled up in front of her and reached out my hands to grasp hers. Looking down at her hands in mine, I began to tear up. I knew what I had to do and I had to keep myself composed.

We continued some small talk as she informed me of further details of her coffee night and new prospects for potential jobs. Most of what she said went in one ear and out the other as I stared down at her hands resting in mine. It wasn't supposed to end this way. These hands were supposed to be mine to hold forever. Her finger was supposed to be the one I'd place the ring upon. Now, that shiny ring sitting in my closet would never grace her hand. I could see her face lighting up in my mind's eye. She'd be overjoyed, experiencing one of the happiest moments in her life as I slid the ring onto her finger. She'd love it. While having never seen it in person, she knew some of the designs I was looking at and I could envision the joy she would emanate. A joy, I would now never see.

"Mia," I began, knowing that if I didn't start soon I would lose my gumption to do so.

I had tried to have this precise conversation the night before, but she wouldn't have it. Before doing so, I asked her to come towards me. I held her in my arms for what seemed like an eternity. I knew that once the words came out, I could never take them back. These words would change everything and I wanted to feel that embrace one last time. If for no other reason than to just offer the sincerest expression of my love and care for her one final time.

Tonight had to be different though. I set my face like a flint knowing how difficult it was going to be. Regardless of the challenge and perceived impossibility, I had to be obedient. I had to do what Jesus was asking me to do, even if it meant dying to myself, especially if it meant dying to myself.

"You know how much I love you right? How I always will and how I would do anything for you?" I said sincerely.

"Yes, and I feel the same way about you, Sean"

"Well, I know I tried to do this last night and I don't want to, but I have to be obedient and I have to do what I feel like I am being led to do. That I am in the way and Jesus wants to do something great in you, that He can't do with me in the picture."

"No, Sean." she began. "You're not in the way. You and I are meant to be together. We were brought together for a reason and this isn't the end."

My heart melted further, but I persisted. "But it is, Mia. It has to be"

"No, we are not ending." she pleaded, now eyes filled with tears.

This back and forth persisted for several minutes with little more being said that, "Yes, it is," and "No, it isn't."

How do I end things with someone who won't accept it? This is hard enough for me to do if she had just accepted it right off the bat, but she hadn't. I was fighting against her. I was fighting against myself; my own wants, and desires and inherently discerned that any slight deviation from the immediate task set before me would end in disobedience.

I didn't have the strength to do this. I didn't have the intestinal fortitude to go against every fiber of my being. I can only characterize my actions and my ability to persist as Christ's strength manifested in me.

After an hour of pleading with her and somehow sticking to my guns, she paused. Eyes glazed over, as if in a trance and said.

"You're right. I need to take care of this thing in my life and I can't be in a relationship and deal with it at the same time."

Now scared to metaphorically spook her, I remained silent as she continued.

"Thank you, Sean. I love you."

Tears still in her eyes, she kissed my forehead and said, "Goodnight."

"Goodnight." I said as she headed downstairs to bed.

CHAPTER 31

Did I Pass?

The hard part was over, or so I thought. The breakup would drag on over the next few months. I was left with a battle within myself. Each day, a siege assaulted my senses; footholds in my mind and heart becoming a very battlefield for the forces within me. Each side launching formidable offenses against the other; both taking casualties, yet, the real carnage revealed as you looked upon the meekness of my heart. I was the human incarnation of cartoon-character lore with good and evil on either shoulder. Stupidly taking input from both sides, I swayed back and forth as a double-minded man. As I had so many other times in my life, I was missing it. I was missing the easy way that God had lain out before me, and instead was taking the path wrought with vines, thistles, and prickly thorns all due to my own lack of faith.

As I internally deliberated, it became abundantly clear that this was about much more than just a relationship. This was about obedience. It was about learning to obey and trust even when I didn't understand it; even when I couldn't see around the next bend in the road. It came down to two very simple questions. Do I want what I think is best for my life or do I want what God says is best for my life? Do I trust Him and His plan that my life is blessed, as He says it is, that He has exceedingly abundantly above for me in my future, or do I trust my own ability? Do I only trust what I can see in front of me? Do I only trust what I can perceive in my own mind? And if so, how plainly shallow is my faith.

Without a doubt, it was the hardest thing I've ever had to do. Total and complete surrender is not an easy lesson to learn. Looking back, it's easy to see with great clarity that I followed what Jesus was instructing me to do. I was obedient in the midst, but it was agonizing beyond description. How I was tormented, stressed, and pained by it all; yet, such emotions gained me nothing.

For so long, I kept a small glimmer of hope that she would come back. Hope that it would all be made whole and the struggle and the pain would be rationalized in an even greater story of love, but it didn't. The day her car was picked up to be shipped, I stopped on the driveway. Early in the morning, I took a moment to stop and reflect. Tears filled my eyes as I wept. I wept because I knew it was over. The finality had set in. There was no more hope for reconciliation. I wept because of what was, what could've been, but also what I now understood would never come to pass.

In fully surrendering and placing my complete and total trust in the Lord's plan for my life, even in an area so important to me, I was assured that what He has for me is so much better than anything I experienced with Mia. Every heartbreak, every tear, every sleepless night would be worth it in knowing my savior cares more for me than I could ever even care for myself.

Through it all, I reminded myself over and over of the story of Abraham and Isaac. How God asked him to sacrifice his own son, and Abraham knowing and believing that God was willing and able to raise his son from the grave was willing to do so; yet, just before taking Isaac's life, God stopped him. It was a test that Abraham passed with flying colors.

I knew instinctively that this was my test. God was capable of restoring it all, should that have been his will. But it was a test and I knew the reward would be great, but contrary to what I hoped for early on, the reward wouldn't be Mia.

CHAPTER 32

The Prize

As a general rule, we are programmed to expect reward. Whether by intrinsic components of our character or learned algorithmic brain patterns, we expect and even anticipate reward. This expectation is only heightened when combined with suffering. It goes contrary to our very nature to experience pain and suffering without reason or retribution. We rally behind the underdog and cheer alongside those who have overcome insurmountable odds.

Sayings like "pain is weakness leaving the body," and "No pain, no gain" train us to rejoice in our suffering. That through this suffering, we are building character. We are being refined and in becoming acutely aware of our own weaknesses, we conquer ourselves. However, the reward we seek is often more tangible. The chiseled physique built only through the discipline of countless hours in the gym and the pain filled muscles that plague us afterward. The diploma we proudly display in our offices after years of all-night study sessions. The number of zeros displayed on our account balances signifying we have achieved success in our right.

I'm no different and there's nothing inherently wrong with those rewards. In fact, it was my expectation following the end of Mia and me. In my mind, there was a new relationship headed my way; a relationship with a woman who would far exceed any of my wildest expectations. She'd be beautiful, loving, caring, and compassionate. She'd be "better." She'd be my reward. She'd make it all worthwhile.

I smiled as I imagined what she'd be like. The attributes she'd portray and the heart she'd have. I believed with complete conviction that God would never ask me to give up something—in this case, Mia—without giving me something better in return. I was impatient, however, and expected her to be "running" me down in quick order. Surprisingly, she wasn't. I went on dates here and there, and even dabbled in the online dating world again, but slowly, a revelation began to surface in my heart. As I wrote these pages, I began to see that the prize Jesus was offering to me was something more eternal than a new relationship.

I still expect the desire of my heart to be fulfilled in the Lord's timing, but it's no longer the number one priority to me. It is no longer what I yearn for in this life. The real prize, the real treasure is something far more precious, and something that could never be taken from me.

This wasn't the first time I'd been tested and assuredly it wouldn't be the last. I was tested time and again. Tested physically during my spinal fusion surgery, tested emotionally during my time at XYZ, and now, I had been tested spiritually in my relationships. My commitment and steadfastness tested with increasing severity along the way.

Was I who I said I was all these years? Did I practice what I preached to others and encouraged them to do? Was I exercising my faith in the way I so vehemently said we all needed to?

Had I continued on in that relationship, the answer would've been no. I would've been nothing, but a hypocrite, nothing but the clanging of a cymbal, nothing but the creaking of a rusty gate.

But after twenty-five years, the revelation finally resonated in my heart. As I write the pages of this book, I see the true prize, the true gift, is not in something temporal. It's not in a van, it's not in a job, it's not in a relationship, and it's not even in life itself. But rather, in understanding the heart of the God we serve. It is recognizing the perfect peace that He offers to us all.

It's plain to see that in each testing I endured it was my weakness common among them all. Each time in my weariness, I had failed. One way or another, whether it was doubt, neglect, or plain lack of trust, I was frail. Yet, in this weakness, strength rose up in and around me. I was pro-

FORGED: MADE STRONG IN WEAKNESS

vided for. Truth was revealed to me to shift my paradigm to another construct; one that as I waited for breakthrough and often grew weary, enabled me to see the fingerprints of a plan far greater than my own. While I doubted, questioned, and at times was even closed off to the obvious movement of God around me, Jesus continued to move. He wasn't inhibited by my lack of faith and continued to put pieces into place to thrust me into my destiny.

As needs and desires of my heart were revealed through heartache and pain, it left an opening where His love could shine through. In my vulnerability, my weaknesses were highlighted. My shortfalls were accentuated. My inabilities and flaws uncovered and made plain. Yet, because those weaknesses were visible, the strength of Christ could be revealed.

Ultimately, I was learning to trust. I was coming to know the character of our Lord. I was coming to trust His promises and see them as the ultimate truths in my life. I was seeing the enormity of His Love for me, but in order for that trust to be manifested, to be cemented I had to experience it for myself.

I was learning to have faith, but also to believe Him for everything in my life, not just my salvation. The reward wasn't just knowing Him, but the revelation that through His character, I could rest in the finished work of Christ. I could be assured that no amount of worry or pleading was going to alter my circumstances for the better or for the worse.

The prize is peace of mind. It's Someone to put my hope in. It's Someone to trust and knowing He won't let me down. I can let go and know beyond a shadow of a doubt He has my best interest at heart. All that's required of me is to give my best and walk out the plan He has laid out for my life, one day at a time.

We come into this world naked and alone, dependent and forced to trust those we see to take care of us and provide. We leave this world naked and alone, yet again, with either an assurance of our future based on faith and trust in one we can't see, or an uncertainty of what lies beyond the depths of the other side. It's a choice we make and if realized, that same faith and trust we aspire to have seconds before our final breath, we can have now. And as such, live a fuller, more peaceful, abundant life right here on earth.

It's a journey; a constant cycle of obeying and exercising faith. As a result, your faith is strengthened. You trust more. Then He asks for a little bit bigger obedience. The stakes increase. There's more on the line. But each time you grow closer to God, you understand His character more, you trust more freely, and it becomes easier to hear His voice and thus accomplish His will.

I'm, by no means, at the end point. I would never claim to have it all figured out, and I am far from perfect. I make mistakes and fall short of the glory of God, every day in word, thought or deed, but while we all take a different path to understanding and knowing the God we serve, if we'll avail ourselves to be used, if we'll make our stories known, we can accelerate the learning for those around us, for those who are willing to hear and receive.

So, what's next for me?

CHAPTER 33

The Vision

I sit with my legs fully straightened out before me. My head resting against the outside rear tire of the Peterbilt grain truck. The upward stretching racks of the grain box cast shade over me and my fellow harvest workers. With my lunchbox to my right, my arm rested upon it, I take a cool drink of water from my thermos as I take in the scene around me. Content to just be sitting in the dirt like a normal person, I can't help but smile.

Our crew consists of my dad, my brother in law, Matt, Phil, the aforementioned pastor-family friend, Shealyn, his daughter, and Uncle Everett. We're a tight knit group who find joy even in the midst of back breaking work.

As we sit, jokes abound and a jovial nature fills us all as the end of harvest draws near. Only a few more days of hard labor and the stress, the push, the grueling work will be finished for the year. For all of us but Dad that is.

As my compadres enjoy their meal and a cold soda, I remark at my ability to sit on this hard, rugged ground comfortably. My legs are straight, no more contractures in my knees. My arms are strong, I can lift them as high as I would ever desire and lifting something as heavy as a weighted lunchbox is no longer a monumental task. I can reach up and take off my ball cap to wipe the sweat from my brow without a second thought. I have no pain, my back is straight, and I can move independently. No longer does the shifting of my position require assistance from others, but I can do it on a whim with no more reason needed than just the desire to do so.

It's perfect. The light breeze and shade creates a backwoods country oasis in the midst of dirt, chaff, and sweat.

"Everett, why don't you try to not break your combine today?" I poke facetiously.

Having spent much of the preceding three days working on his machine after an unsuspecting rock made mincemeat out of the insides of his combine, the ongoing joke was his ability to find and pick up rocks even in the most unlikely of places.

"No promises there, Sean. I know I'm letting you down yet again." he said good naturedly as a spry smile spread across his face.

"Well, after lunch, Everett, why don't you cut over on the Northeast side of the patch up the draw and I'll go back and forth on this side and we can keep the trucks here centrally?" Dad chimed in, offering my uncle a respite from the teasing he always endured, from me especially.

"You got it, boss!"

We didn't usually stop for lunch like this. Back in my younger days, we would. Shutting all the equipment down at noon, we would gather around to "shoot the breeze" and take a break from the confines of a cramped cab. We ceased that practice several years ago, however, realizing over the course of harvest, that daily hour break was costing us significant productivity. But today, with the end only a couple days away, it was the perfect way to unwind. The day was scorching and with morale at its peak, taking some time to enjoy it was just fine by me.

"At some point this afternoon, we will want to grab the old international truck too." Dad continued.

The truck sat about a mile away as the crow flies. We'd be finishing the field we were currently harvesting in a couple hours, and would need the truck in order to move equipment to our next location.

"So Sean or Matt, if you want to give Shealyn or somebody a ride over there later, then we can shuffle vehicles back and forth so…"

He was interrupted mid-sentence by the sound of scuffling in the dirt.

Before he could regain his train of thought. he realized, instinctively, like the reflexes of a leg, at his saying so, I had risen to my feet. In the quickest and smoothest of motions, I bounded to my feet and took off running in the direction of the international truck.

My right foot dug into the soft silt below. My green and grey Nike fly knit shoes bent at mid-foot as the ball of my foot twisted and pushed off against the ground. As my foot turned, it created a dimple of ridges, miniscule waves in the dirt only to be disrupted nanoseconds later by the plume of dust left behind as I jetted around the back end of the truck.

"Well, I didn't necessarily mean right this second…" his voice trailing off knowing I was clearly already out of earshot.

My fellow harvesters stood and moved around the corner of the truck to see me at a dead sprint making my way towards the International.

The words smile and joy don't begin to touch the faintest edges of the emotion overflowing from the innermost caverns of my being in that very moment. Arms stretched out wide like a soccer player who just scored the winning goal in the World Cup. I continued at top speed away from the now bewildered bystanders I sat with only moments ago.

As I ran, the dirt beneath my feet, kicking up plumes of dust with every methodical stride, the ground takes on a life of its own. Each step was a physical embodiment of the mold I was cast into. My grandfather worked this land, my father worked this land, and this farm was made possible because of the actions of generations before me. My entire family poured blood, sweat, and tears into this enterprise to make it what it is.

In the same way, they've poured that same heartfelt passion into me. I get to experience the generational blessing of their devotion to God, because they set their faces to what they believed in, the ultimate truth. Under His guidance, they shaped and provided this mold for me to be cast into.

In their commitment to God and family, they demonstrated that the message is the person; how important it is to judge others by their worth and not by their ability. To withstand popular approval or a serious blow and hold fast to what is right; to never give up, to never quit trying, to be steadfast, to always believe, and when all else fails to just stand.

Continuing my sprint, I slow as I approached the dirt road. Scaling the embankment, and jumping into the middle of the road, my feet meet the soft powdery surface that is the dirt road in late August. Hammering my feet into the ground with all the force, my now able body can muster, a billow of dust erupts around me, enveloping me, and coats every inch of my body in a thin layer of dirt.

Across the road, I increase my speed back to a brisk run. Not sprinting, but a quick, deliberate pace. Another half a mile and I'd be there. I'm in no hurry, though. I am content to just run. I have waited all my life for this moment. The joy in my face and heart palpable in every step I take; a joy that is magnified because of what I endured to get here; the sleepless nights, the tears shed, the trials and tribulations thrown my way; all of it the liquefying and the heating of my very nature.

Ascending a long sloping hill, my legs begin to ache. My thighs burn and muscles cramp from the heat. I'm out of breath and thirsty for water, but I ignore its screams and pleas, I rejoice amidst the pain, knowing that the pain I feel is because of my ability to run. A pain that is more precious to me than gold.

With each stride, the pain dulls. Content to be running my race the old 1970s international truck comes into view. Approaching it, I open the driver side door and climb in. Cushioned by the plush seat, I place my hands on the wheel, but before starting the engine, I reopen the door, climb out setting my feet in the grass once again, I pause, and then climb back in, just because I can.

Starting the engine, I step on the brake and the clutch while releasing the emergency brake. With a slow labored turn, the engine sputters to life. Shifting into second, I release the brake and slowly let out the clutch while simultaneously gently depressing the accelerator. Slowly, contentedly, and with that same smile on my face, I pull onto the road.

The joy I have in this vision is the same joy I have in anticipation of that moment. It's something that can never be taken away from me. It's not based on my current circumstances. It's not based on my mood, but rather a trust in my Heavenly Father. An assurance that, one day, I will run. One day, I will stretch my arms out to my side, with a smile on my face, and feel the wind blow past me as I look towards the sky with awe and wonder. It's a joy that isn't based solely on my ability to walk and run, which I obviously look forward to with great excitement and anticipation, but more so, based on the unchanging nature of my God.

A joy that is cemented in my eternal destiny which enables me to live today with that same joy and contentment I would have if I ran to that truck yesterday. Nothing can take it away from me. No calamity, no plague, and no human can affect or alter that assurance.

As the old truck rounds the corner and passes out of sight, the roar of the engine can barely be heard above the rustling of the trees. A trail of dust continues to pass from left to right as the truck slowly follows along the old dirt road. The dust rises ever higher, dissipating, and lessening in origin the further away it gets.

That cloud of dust is my life. Here today and gone tomorrow. While every detail may not transpire in the way I would've authored it, I can rest assured knowing it was good. I can rest assured knowing I led a life of love. I had faith. I trusted. I endeavored to exhibit humility, inner constancy, and to cultivate a wise heart. I purposed to aim for something higher than happiness, to be of service to the world, and to value the ripening virtues of those who have learned from joy and pain. Most of all, I will have been prepared for what comes next. I will have lived. I will have not let anything stop me from experiencing everything this life has to offer.

What happens between now and that last cloud of dust? I don't know exactly. I know there will be more hammering, more refining, and more blessing to experience. There will be trials and there will be indescribable favor. I'll laugh, I'll cry, I'll rejoice in victory, and experience the agony of loss and disappointment; but through it all, I will have been prepared. I will be sharpened as a blade and when called upon to fight, I'll be ready, a hand crafted weapon; simply put, *Forged*.

About the Author

Sean Neal is a fighter. He doesn't let anything stop him. He lives life with a ferocity unmatched by even the staunchest of athletes. He's fiercely competitive and views this life as a competition, one in which he is determined to win, resolute to continue climbing, taking footholds, and holding his ground in the battle to become the best version of himself.

This attitude didn't just simply appear, however. It wasn't bestowed upon him. Instead, it had to be built. It had to be hardened and molded and his very nature cast into it. How? Through the trials and tribulations of this life. He knows what it feels like to just want to give up; like it's not worth it. After being told he wouldn't live past age ten by an ill-informed doctor, he was later diagnosed with a neuromuscular disease known as Spinal Muscular Atrophy. He experienced great physical and emotional pain and had multiple surgeries by the age of twelve. Yet, his story isn't a dismal one. Instead, it's about love, hope, and victory.

Through an unshakable faith and belief in Jesus, he views himself as a kingdom warrior for Christ. Through his eyes, you would not see a disabled man, but rather one who rises to the occasion. His greatest pride is seeing the love of Jesus demonstrated in others and spending time with his family and those he loves.

He was born the son of a farmer and grew up with a passion for agriculture. Being physically unable to partake in many aspects of the farm, he pursued finance and excelled academically. He graduated from Washington State University with a degree in finance after which, he pursued a career as a financial advisor. Following his stint with Edward Jones Investments, he found an opportunity to work for his alma mater, where he currently works as a financial reporting manager. His real passion, however, is the farm and sharing the love of Christ with audiences of varying kinds.

He has spoken to over 25,000 people and has been the featured speaker at Washington State University, Eastern Washington University, Washington FFA, Washington FCCLA as well as churches and youth groups. His speeches are high energy, full of laughter, and reflective as he shares his life story. To find out more about Sean, please visit:

www.seannealspeaks.com
www.facebook.com/seannealFAN
www.twitter.com/seannealspeaks